THE CONSCIOUS PARENT'S GUIDE TO

Executive Functioning Disorder

BOOST CONCENTRATION

GET ORGANIZED

IMPROVE SELF-CONTROL

A mindful approach for helping your child focus and learn

Rebecca Branstetter, PhD

adamsmedia

Avon, Massachusetts

DEDICATION

To my husband, Steven, thank you, as always, for your continued support. There is no one else in this would I would want by my side to raise our little girls. To my two amazing daughters, thank you for teaching me more about parenting than any course ever could! You have also taught me how to truly enjoy life. Seeing the world from your eyes and learning with you has been the greatest gift.

Published by
Adams Media, a division of F+W Media, Inc.
57 Littlefield Street, Avon, MA 02322. U.S.A.
www.adamsmedia.com

Contains material adapted from *The Everything® Parent's Guide to Children with Executive Functioning Disorder* by Rebecca Branstetter, PhD, copyright © 2014 by F+W Media, Inc., ISBN 10: 1-4405-6685-2, ISBN 13: 978-1-4405-6685-1.

ISBN 10: 1-4405-9432-5
ISBN 13: 978-1-4405-9432-8
eISBN 10: 1-4405-9433-3
eISBN 13: 978-1-4405-9433-5

Printed in the United States of America.

10 9 8 7 6 5 4 3 2 1

This book is intended as general information only, and should not be used to diagnose or treat any health condition. In light of the complex, individual, and specific nature of health problems, this book is not intended to replace professional medical advice. The ideas, procedures, and suggestions in this book are intended to supplement, not replace, the advice of a trained medical professional. Consult your physician before adopting any of the suggestions in this book, as well as about any condition that may require diagnosis or medical attention. The author and publisher disclaim any liability arising directly or indirectly from the use of this book.

Many of the designations used by manufacturers and sellers to distinguish their products are claimed as trademarks. Where those designations appear in this book and F+W Media, Inc. was aware of a trademark claim, the designations have been printed with initial capital letters.

Cover design by Alexandra Artiano.

This book is available at quantity discounts for bulk purchases.
For information, please call 1-800-289-0963.

Contents

CHAPTER 5: RESPONSE INHIBITION: TEACHING YOUR CHILD TO CONTROL IMPULSES 73

CHAPTER 6: FOCUS: EVERYDAY MINDFULNESS 85

CHAPTER 7: TIME MANAGEMENT: STRENGTHENING YOUR CHILD'S INTERNAL CLOCK 95

CHAPTER 8: WORKING MEMORY: HOLD THAT THOUGHT 107

Introduction

Chances are, if you picked up this book, either you have been told that your child has executive functioning challenges or you have heard the term *executive functioning* used in the field of education and are curious what all the buzz is about. Either way, you've come to the right book.

Children have their own sets of strengths and weaknesses. In the same way that some children take to reading like ducks to water, there are some children who take to planning, organization, self-discipline, self-control, and time management with very little direct instruction. On the flip side, there are some children who need extra support in reading, or with executive functioning tasks, and they will require more intensive interventions to be as successful as some of their classmates. Fortunately, there are strategies that work for children and adolescents with executive functioning challenges, many of which you will learn in this book.

Knowing that children learn and grow at different paces helps parents become more patient with the struggling child. The aim of this book is twofold: first, to help you better understand where you should set the bar for your child to master executive functioning skills, and, second, to guide you in a mindful approach that lets you tailor strategies for him to help him reach that bar and achieve more success and less stress from his efforts. So let's get started!

 **CHAPTER 1**

Conscious Parenting

Being a conscious parent is all about building strong, sustainable bonds with your children through mindful living and awareness. Traditional power-based parenting techniques that promote compliance and obedience can disconnect you from your children. Conscious parenting, on the other hand, helps you develop a positive emotional connection with your child. You acknowledge your child's unique self and attempt to empathize with his way of viewing the world. Through empathetic understanding and tolerance you create a safe environment where your child feels that his ideas and concerns are truly being heard. When you find yourself in a stressful situation with your child, rather than reacting with anger or sarcasm, remember that conscious parenting reminds you to take a step back, reflect, and look for a peaceful solution—one that honors your child's individuality and motivations. This approach benefits all children, especially children with executive functioning deficits. Children and adolescents who need support in planning, organizing, managing their time, and regulating their behavior and emotions can be challenging to parent. Fortunately, the mutual frustration felt between children with executive functioning difficulties and their parents can be lessened through conscious parenting practices.

Adopting the conscious parenting philosophy can relieve your stress and improve your child's self-image. The strong bond built between you and your child, along with your own calm, respectful attitude, help him to develop positive behavior patterns. One of the most powerful ways to teach your child how to self-regulate behaviors, emotions, and goals is to lead by example. By adopting a conscious mindset and practicing mindful parenting practices, you are actually modeling many of the skills he will need to improve his executive functioning.

The Benefits of Conscious Parenting

Conscious parenting isn't a set of rules or regulations that you must follow, but rather a system of beliefs. Conscious parents engage and connect with their children, using mindful and positive discipline rather than punishment. They try to be present when they're spending time with their children, avoiding distractions such as TV and social media. Conscious parents respect their children and accept them as they are. The most important part of conscious parenting is building an emotional connection with your child so you can understand the underlying reasons for her behavior.

> Conscious parenting is about listening with full attention, and embracing a nonjudgmental acceptance of yourself and your child. As you engage in the act of *becoming*, you will discover a heightened sense of emotional awareness of yourself and your child, a clearer self-regulation in the parenting relationship, and a greater compassion for yourself and your child.

Conscious parenting brings with it a number of benefits, including improved communication, stronger relationships, and a feeling of greater happiness and satisfaction in life. Some of these benefits appear immediately, while others take some time to emerge. The benefits of conscious parenting and mindfulness are a result of making this philosophy a part of your daily life. With practice, conscious parenting becomes an integral part of who and how you are in the world, and can then become a central part of who your child is as well.

SELF-AWARENESS AND SELF-CONTROL

One of the first benefits of conscious parenting that you (and your child) will see is a heightened awareness of yourself and your inner life, including your emotions, thoughts, and feelings. As you become more aware of these various forces moving within you, you can begin to watch them rise without being at their mercy. For example, when you are aware that you are becoming angry, you have a choice about whether to act from that anger or attend to that feeling directly. You will start to notice the things that tend to set you off—your triggers—and be able to anticipate your emotions before they have a hold on you.

Mindfulness is the practice of being attentive in every moment, and noticing what is taking place both inside and outside of you without passing judgment. It is the practice of purposefully seeing your thoughts, emotions, experiences, and surroundings as they arise. Simply put, mindfulness is the act of paying attention.

As you become more skilled at noticing the thoughts and feelings that arise, you will begin to notice them more quickly, maybe even before they start to affect your actions. This awareness is itself a powerful tool. It opens up the possibility of saying, "Hey, I'm pretty mad right now . . . " instead of yelling at somebody you care about because you were upset about something else. The practice can do exactly the same thing for your child, helping her to learn to communicate about her feelings rather than just react from that place of emotion. As with most things, children learn this best by seeing it modeled by the adults in their lives.

Often, you may notice that your emotions carry with them a sense of urgency. As you feel the impulse to do something arise within you, you will be able to identify the forces driving that sense of "I need to do something." They could be, for example, the thoughts that come up as you watch a three-year-old put on her own shoes. Your mind might be buzzing with impatience, and the thought "I need to put her shoes on for her because she's taking forever" arises. When you notice this thought, rather than immediately acting on it, you can check in with yourself and act intentionally instead of just reacting. This practice of noticing creates a certain amount of mental space in which you can examine the thought or feeling itself rather than being moved to act by it.

WELL-BEING

Conscious parents understand that all they do and say over the course of each day *matters*. It is a sense of the *now*, being present in the moment without regard or worry for the past or future. When you become more mindful, you may find that you become more accepting of the things in life that you can't change and experience less stress. The net result is greater satisfaction and enjoyment of whatever each day has to offer. This sense of well-being offers a satisfaction and contentment in knowing that you are who you are intended to be, doing precisely what you are designed for in the moment.

As human beings, we each possess the tools for contributing something of value. Assess your gifts and talents—those personality traits and skills that make you unique—and determine how to employ them to enhance your parenting. If you take a full account of yourself—good, bad, and indifferent—and *own* the sum total of your individual experience, you are taking the first step toward conscious parenting.

EMPATHY

The awareness you gain as a conscious parent has the practical purpose of redefining your perception of yourself and your compassionate understanding of your child. When you understand how your child experiences the world and how she learns, you can communicate in ways that really reach her. Conscious parenting encourages you to view your behavior through your child's point of view and to mold your reactions to meet her needs. This largely happens through modeling, or teaching through example. Doing so allows you to pass on the values and lessons that are important to you, regardless of your beliefs.

It is particularly important to develop an awareness of how your child feels when she has trouble regulating her behaviors or feelings. Children with executive functioning weaknesses usually do the best they can with the tools they have, but are often told by others that they need to do better, or that they are not motivated. However, in most cases, if these children had the tools to do well, they would. The job of a conscious parent is to meet your child where she is and teach her the tools to focus, complete tasks, and be organized, while understanding that these tasks do not naturally come easily for her. Using empathy and having an understanding that she needs coaching on tasks that other children her age may not need will go a long way toward helping your child feel supported.

ACCEPTANCE AND VALIDATION

Your child relies upon you and your family to provide a solid foundation of self-esteem. Equipped with a strong sense of self-worth, your child will be better prepared to enter into a life that will likely present many challenges. Much of your time and energy will be expended in raising, counseling, and disciplining your child in ways that she will understand. It is important to try to equalize those occasions by reinforcing your love and appreciation of her gifts and talents.

Giving Your Child Full Attention

All too often people multitask their way through the day. This is a common coping mechanism you have probably developed as a means of juggling the many projects, tasks, errands, and obligations that you are responsible for. But it splits your attention in ways that distract your mind and lessen the quality of your attention, causing your work and social interactions to suffer.

To avoid this becoming an issue between you and your child (and to model the kind of focus and engagement that you want your child to use), make sure to practice engaged listening when you are at home with your family. This means setting aside other distractions, making eye contact, and giving the speaker (in this case, your child) your full attention.

Even if you set down what you are doing and are looking at your child, check in with yourself. Is your mind focused on what he is saying, or is it still planning, scheduling, remembering, projecting, or worrying? It is very easy to only half-listen, and this can be especially true when it comes to listening to children.

Multitasking is neurologically impossible. When you try to multitask, what you actually end up doing is rapidly switching between tasks. Each time you do so, you lose efficiency and concentration, so stop trying! Do one thing at a time so you can do it with your whole brain, then move on to the next.

The stories your child tells are not always very interesting or relevant to your adult life. The idea behind active listening is not that you suddenly care about what everyone else brought to school for Show and Tell today; it's that you care about your child, and he wants to tell you the funny, strange, or interesting things that he experienced that day. The important part of this interaction is that your child wants to share his joy, curiosity, and interests with you. He wants to interact with you and share parts of himself and his life with you, and this is one of the ways he can do that. Don't miss out on this gift, even if the subject itself bores you. You'll be surprised by the interest you may develop in these things as you listen to your child talk. When a person you love cares about something, it becomes easier to see that "something" through his eyes and come to appreciate it all the more.

Understanding Behavior

Children and adolescents who have difficulties in executive functioning are often labeled "lazy," "forgetful," "inconsistent," or "lost." Their challenges often lead to difficulties in the classroom, such as forgetting to turn in assignments, making careless errors, and having difficulties staying on-task and keeping up with the pace of the class. At home, a child may experience challenges as well. She might lose her belongings, have trouble remembering routines, fail to complete chores, or have emotional reactions that are extreme for the situation. Difficulties with executive functioning can also impact social relationships. For example, if a child forgets to meet with her friend, says something without thinking first, loses something she borrowed, or is constantly late to meet up, there can be friction in friendships. The good news is that the skills these children have difficulties with can also be taught.

It is understandably frustrating to have a child who is constantly leaving belongings everywhere, forgetting to turn in that homework you spent hours helping with, or procrastinating for hours on end. But just remember that no child wants to fail to meet parental expectations. Sometimes it isn't a motivation issue; it's that the child lacks the skill set to be successful. The first step to teaching your child the skills she needs to pay attention, follow through, and become independent is to understand her behavior through conscious parenting.

What does it mean to be a conscious parent of a child with executive functioning problems? Conscious parenting means different things to different people, but the essence is that you are making parenting choices with the intention of nurturing your child and putting your relationship first. Instead of focusing on how to control your child's behaviors and feelings, conscious parents seek to understand and get at the *root* of the behavior or feeling.

For children with difficulties independently meeting goals, traditional parenting tactics of rewarding "good" behavior and punishing "bad" behavior can backfire. Often, the child does not yet have the skill set to meet expectations, and punishment then leads to resentment and shame. Not that there aren't appropriate times for rewards and punishments; however, you should take into consideration whether the problem behavior is a "will problem" or a "skill problem." Most often, there is a lagging skill that needs to be taught. Becoming your child's partner in understanding the challenge and collaborating on solving it together can strengthen your relationship with your child.

To illustrate the pitfalls of using only rewards and punishments to change behavior, imagine that someone put a difficult calculus problem in front of you (presuming you are not a mathematician or calculus teacher) and said, "If you do this, you get $1,000, and if you don't, you have to pay me $1,000." If you never learned calculus, you are getting punished for something that is simply beyond your skill set.

It is useful for parents to keep in mind that being a conscious parent is not a destination, but a journey. When you get stressed, overwhelmed, and frustrated, it is difficult to be present, respectful, and reflective before acting in response to your child's behavior. Just as you want to be patient with your child as she learns new skills, it is worth reminding yourself that you are also on your own journey and should be patient with yourself.

 **CHAPTER 2**

What Is Executive Functioning?

In order to be an advocate for your child and empathize with his challenges, you should have a solid background in what executive functioning is. At first, the term *executive functioning* sounds like something that belongs in the boardroom. That's probably because the word *executive* evokes an image of a person doing all of the tasks necessary to be successful in a business—managing time, being organized, changing course when needed, strategizing, and thinking ahead. But this book is not about teaching your child to be the next CEO of a major corporation. It is about teaching your child to be the CEO of his own learning.

Defining Executive Functioning

Many formal definitions of executive functioning exist in the research on the psychology of learning. In general, there is consensus that executive functioning skills are all of the cognitive skills needed to regulate your thinking, feeling, and behavior, often to reach a goal. What is important to know is that executive functioning skills are needed for all the other cognitive processes as well, such as memory, attention, motor skills, verbalizing, visualizing, and completing learning tasks. Executive functioning skills are also used to regulate emotions. Put another way, if the brain is the engine of learning and self-regulation, executive functioning is the driver of that engine.

Definitions of executive functioning skills often include the following basic functions:

- **Task Initiation:** Stopping what you are doing and starting a new task.

- **Response Inhibition:** Keeping yourself from acting impulsively, in order to achieve a goal.

- **Focus:** Directing your attention, keeping your focus, and managing distractions while working on a task.

- **Time Management:** Understanding and feeling the passage of time, planning good use of your time, and avoiding procrastination behaviors.

- **Working Memory:** Holding information in your mind long enough to do something with it (remember it, process it, act on it).

- **Flexibility:** Being able to shift your ideas and plans in changing conditions.

- **Self-Regulation:** Being able to reflect on your actions and behaviors and make needed changes to reach a goal.

- **Emotional Self-Control:** Managing your emotions and reflecting on your feelings in order to keep yourself from engaging in impulsive behaviors.

O **Task Completion:** Sustaining your levels of attention and energy to see a task to the end.

O **Organization:** Keeping track and taking care of your belongings (personal belongings, schoolwork) and maintaining order in your personal space.

Research on executive functioning has burgeoned in the past twenty years, often including brain-based neuroscience. The region of the brain that has been associated with the executive functions, such as planning, organizing, shifting attention, problem-solving, and self-control, is the prefrontal cortex, or the frontal lobe.

Part of being a mindful parent is to simply notice your child's executive functioning strengths and weaknesses, not to judge them as "good" or "bad." His skills are where they are at this moment in time. Parents can help children build their executive functioning skills while at the same time being respectful of where they are in their journey. By doing so, you are strengthening the relationship with your child, because he will feel that you are accepting him and supporting him at the same time.

The prefrontal cortex continues to develop well into early adulthood. The executive functions are among the last to fully mature in child development. As such, you should not expect your school-age children and adolescents to have fully developed executive functioning skills. The region of the brain that is responsible for executive control is a work in progress. Knowing this fact can help parents and teachers become more patient with students who struggle in these areas.

BEING A PARENT: THE ULTIMATE TEST IN EXECUTIVE FUNCTIONING

To better understand executive functioning skills in your child, think of ways you use executive functioning in your own life. At times, parents may feel like the CEOs of their families. Parents organize schedules, shift plans when needed, put aside things they'd rather do in favor of higher priorities, and plan for the present as well as the future. In fact, the skills used to manage your household are the very same executive functioning skills you are likely trying to develop in your child.

For example, when you are planning a family trip, you may talk to family members about where you want to go, then narrow down your choices by price, weather, and availability. Perhaps you research how to get there by car or plane, line up pet sitters and house sitters, ask for time off work, and try to get some things done early so you don't have a huge backlog when you get back. You might put aside money for the trip, or make a plan for paying off credit card bills later. As the trip gets closer, you might make a list of what you need to bring and begin packing. All of these planning, organizing, thinking-ahead, and anticipating skills are executive functions. You use them every day, whether you are aware of them or not.

THE "BOSS IN YOUR BRAIN"

When explaining executive functioning to children, it may be helpful to use imagery. Have your child think of a tiny man or woman in the front of her brain (to represent the frontal lobe) being "the boss" of her brain. The "boss" tells her what to pay attention to, what to do first, what to remember, and so on. Children and adolescents like being the boss of things! For some reason, when you tell a kid she gets to be the boss of planning out her science project, it resonates better than telling her she is "responsible" for planning out her science project.

Using imagery with children is a good way to help them understand complex concepts such as executive functioning. Find a metaphor or image that works for your child, perhaps based on his interests. For example, if your child likes trains, you can say, "Like a train going up a steep track, it takes you a while to get going on your homework. But once you do, you are fast and do a great job!"

You might carry the boss analogy further to explain when your child is lagging in some of the executive functions. For example, if she forgets to complete a part of her homework, you might say, "Looks like the boss in your brain was on a break! Let's look at these directions again." For children and adolescents who are sensitive to feedback, this can be a nice way to alert them to their challenges in a friendly way.

"Smooth Sailors" versus "Boat Rockers"

Children all grow and learn at different paces. Some kids learn very quickly, and others require more adult guidance. There are some children who seem to sail smoothly through learning how to self-regulate, self-monitor, and work independently. These are kids who do need reminders when they are learning something new, but after a few times, they catch on to the routine and need fewer and fewer reminders. They may also be innovative in problem-solving. When faced with a new task, they might spontaneously come up with a faster, better, or new way to solve the problem, without much adult guidance at all. They tend to be able to put aside temptations (TV, social media, playing outside) in order to finish tasks such as homework or chores.

Of course, even the smoothest of sailors still need adult intervention to become skilled in completing tasks such as remembering chores, completing homework well, remembering to turn in homework, catching careless mistakes in their schoolwork, planning ahead for long-term projects and tests, turning off screens in favor of focusing on a project, and expressing their feelings instead of acting out. They just need *less* adult intervention than kids who have challenges in executive functioning, and they tend to learn from their mistakes and file away strategies to use more readily next time.

On the other hand, there are the "boat rockers." It seems that no matter how many times you remind them about something, they inevitably forget it. They work in bursts and are known for their patterns of ups and downs. One week they are on top of their work, and the next they are losing things, getting stuck, and procrastinating all over again. They may become excited at the suggestion of a new strategy, try it for a while, and then lose steam and go back to ineffective strategies. They can't seem to help themselves and are often disappointed in their performance. They frequently want to do better, but they feel that they can't. Sometimes they give up easily. They require a lot of adult intervention to do tasks that perhaps their siblings or friends can do independently.

PARENTING A "BOAT ROCKER"

Parenting a "boat rocker" can be trying, even if you tend to be a very patient person. What seems like common sense is often lacking in a child with executive functioning difficulties. You may find yourself getting frustrated because it seems so obvious that when your child works all weekend on a project, he will surely remember to take it to school on Monday. You know that something could take ten minutes if your child just focused on it. Instead, you are in disbelief that it ends up taking two hours. This is partially because parents can forget what it is like to learn something new and challenging.

For children with executive functioning deficits, it can be a real challenge to get started and keep focus. In order to have more empathy and patience with your child, just think of the last time you had to learn something new or perform a complex task, such as programming the DVR, fixing a flat tire, learning a new computer program, or reading a complicated tax document. Learning something new or doing something difficult can be frustrating. If someone helps you through the process, it can ease your frustration. If someone stands over you and tells you that it should only take ten minutes, so just get it done, chances are it will increase your frustration.

Sometimes you may find it hard not to think of your child's difficulties as solely a motivation issue. This is because your child may be inconsistent in her skills. But inconsistency does not mean that she completes tasks when motivated and doesn't when unmotivated. It just means that there are certain conditions in which her executive functioning skills are being supported. Your job is to figure out what those conditions are and apply them to the situations in which she is less successful.

But how do you explain when your child is having challenges with tasks or routines that are not new? Why can't he just remember the routine? You might find yourself saying things like, "I shouldn't have to remind you to do this! We do this every day!" The fact is, if your child has executive functioning challenges, he may still struggle with tasks, even though they are daily and routine. Just think of a habit that you have tried to change, such as quitting smoking or exercising more. It can be challenging to change, and old habits die hard. There are inevitably setbacks, even though you *know* what to do.

Typical Development

For all learning and behavior in children and adolescents, there is no one age at which a skill is mastered. Rather, there is a range of what is "typical" for most children and adolescents. To illustrate, think of a classroom of six-year-olds all lined up for a race. It is not expected that they will all finish at the exact same time, right? They take off running, and only a few kids finish way ahead or way behind the other kids. The majority of kids will trickle in around the middle of the pack. The same goes for developing executive functioning skills. The age at which a child is able to do a task independently will vary. However, there are several ways you can tell whether your child is accomplishing tasks in the middle of the pack of same-age peers.

Parents with more than one child have the advantage of being able to compare their children's development. One child may have been quick to learn how to clean her room, while her sibling may reach that milestone earlier or later. One child may have stronger abilities to focus than the other. Parents can also gauge their child's development by talking to other parents with children the same age about what tasks their children can do independently.

Parents can also get a sense of how their child's executive functioning skills are coming along by asking their child's teacher. The teacher has a classroom of students the same age, has most likely taught the same age group for a while, and has a good sense of the typical range for skill development. At parent-teacher conferences, if issues around organization, time management, homework completion, or the like are raised, ask if the issue is more severe in your child than in other kids your child's age or if the issue is fairly typical.

Be careful about doing too much comparison with your friends' children's development. Children develop at different rates, so don't get too worried if a peer is advancing in a skill and your child is not. Childhood is not a competition. Use the observation about peers' development as information about which skills may need to be built in your child, and use other parents as resources for how to encourage certain skills.

See Appendix A for a list of executive functioning skills that are expected from children and adolescents at different stages of development.

WHEN CHALLENGES ARISE

Though not all children will develop executive functioning skills at the same time, there are times when children are lagging in their skills so much that it interferes with daily functioning. If there are daily frustrations with your child's ability to complete tasks that she should be able to complete at her age, then you might have a "boat rocker" on your hands. This is not to say that your child is *intentionally* rocking the boat. It just means that the development of self-regulation skills such as organizing, managing time, learning independently, and initiating and completing tasks is not coming naturally to your child.

DELAY OR DISORDER?

Sometimes a child's executive functioning skills are delayed, and with some targeted intervention she will catch up to her peers. For example, a child just entering middle school may be struggling with how to remember which books to bring to which class, now that she has more than one teacher. A teacher or parent may provide some strategies or supports for the child and she will get the hang of the multiple transitions after a few months.

At other times, delays can be chronic. A child may constantly be behind her peers in executive functioning skills. For example, a child may tend to function a grade level or two behind throughout her school career. Parents may notice her consistently acting more like a younger child in her skills. Or a parent of a child with executive functioning challenges in the area of organization may notice that even at the end of middle school, the child needs her backpack checked every morning to make sure she has her homework, while most middle-school students no longer require that level of monitoring. The child with executive functioning delays seems to show an independence level of a younger child. At times, these delays are so severe that an assessment is conducted to uncover the causes or to seek eligibility for special services at the school.

Assessment of Executive Functioning Difficulties

The skills that fall under the umbrella of executive functioning are varied, and so are the types of assessments that are used to evaluate these skills. However, there are several common components of a quality assessment: observations, interviews, rating scales, and direct assessment.

Getting a high-quality assessment of your child is often the first step in uncovering the reasons for your child's executive functioning challenges. It can sometimes be a confusing and lengthy process, but it is worth finding a high-quality assessor to walk you through it. You can get recommendations from your pediatrician, or if your child is school-age, you can start by consulting with the school psychologist.

OBSERVATIONS

One of the best ways to gauge a child's application of executive functioning skills is to observe the child in the school setting. Observations are important because sometimes children do very well in one-on-one testing situations and their executive functioning challenges may not be demonstrated in that setting. When a child is being tested by one adult in a quiet testing room, it is highly structured and there are no distractions. This may be where your child shines, so getting a view of how he functions in a larger, less structured environment such as a classroom is an important part of the assessment.

Observations also take into account the environment in which the child is expected to function. A child may demonstrate executive functioning challenges in one setting but not another. For example, in a highly structured and organized classroom, the child may be able to function better than in a loosely run classroom.

INTERVIEWS

In assessing executive functioning skills, it is important to get the perspectives of many different people who observe the child in different settings. Parents, of course, have the broadest perspective on their children's behavior. They have an understanding of how skills have developed (or not developed) over time, and can provide many anecdotes that give the assessor an understanding of the day-to-day challenges that may arise. Assessors may gather information about your child by having you describe his development, complete surveys about your concerns, or go through a checklist of executive functioning strengths and areas of need.

The assessor's checklist of skills that children and adolescents are expected to do includes such areas as homework, chores, test-taking, studying, organization of belongings, and goal-setting. The assessor will often seek examples of times when these areas are challenging for your child and times when they are not. This information is helpful both to understand the challenges and to generate recommendations for addressing them.

RATING SCALES

In addition to the qualitative information obtained from observation and anecdote, a valuable quantitative assessment can be obtained using rating scales. Rating scales are surveys that describe a number of behaviors and ask the rater to mark how frequently the behavior occurs (never, sometimes, often, always). The behaviors surveyed depend on which rating scale is used, but most likely will be behaviors associated with executive functioning skills (planning, organizing, focus) and social-emotional problems that may interfere with executive functioning (depression, anxiety). Surveys may also include items about your child's behavioral and emotional strengths. Assessors will likely also give rating scales to your child's teacher to get a view of his behavior across different settings.

DIRECT ASSESSMENT

Executive functioning skills are intertwined with a number of cognitive skills. For example, children with auditory-processing problems (difficulties attending to and remembering information they hear) can have executive functioning problems. They might not follow directions correctly or make careless mistakes because they miss information. Children with learning disabilities can also show executive functioning problems. If you better understand how your child learns, then you will better understand his executive functioning. This can be accomplished through direct assessment.

According to special-education law, public school districts are responsible for identifying children with disabilities. Even if your child is in private school, you may be entitled to an evaluation with the school district free of charge. Contact your local school district of residence for more information.

There are a few different names for the direct assessment process. In school settings, this is called a psychoeducational assessment. In clinical settings, it may be called a neuropsychological assessment. There are variations in the name (neurobehavioral evaluation, educational assessment, psychological assessment), but the core features are similar. The assessor works directly with the child by administering a variety of educational and psychological tests to see how the child learns. There is no one test for executive functioning problems or learning and attention problems. Each test is a data point, and they are all put together with qualitative information to form a profile of the child. Think of an assessment as a snapshot of your child's learning skills. It doesn't represent the entire scrapbook of his life. This snapshot can be the first data point in a series of points that will eventually form a clearer picture of your child's functioning. The assessor will typically evaluate the following areas:

○ **Intelligence:** how your child solves new problems on his own

○ **Information processing:** how your child learns best

○ **Attention and executive functioning:** focus, stop-and-think skills, multitasking (task-switching) abilities, sticking with mundane tasks, following complex directions with distractions

○ **Academic skills:** reading, writing, math

○ **Social, emotional, and behavioral functioning:** how your child thinks and feels about himself, how others view his behavior and emotions

Executive Functioning: "The Big Umbrella"

Since executive functioning deficits are a symptom of a number of disorders, it may be helpful to think about them as an umbrella under which many different disorders fall. Under the umbrella are many different childhood and adolescent disorders, but there are a few that are most commonly associated with executive functioning difficulties. This is not an exhaustive list of the disorders that may cause executive functioning problems, but it does include the most prevalently diagnosed ones.

ATTENTION DEFICIT HYPERACTIVITY DISORDER (ADHD)

No two students with ADHD are exactly alike. However, students with ADHD tend to fall into three different categories: those whose primary symptom is inattention, those whose primary symptom is hyperactivity/impulsivity, and those who exhibit both inattention and hyperactivity. Regardless of the subtype of ADHD (inattentive, hyperactive, or combined type), they frequently share common features when it comes to challenges with executive functioning.

There is strong evidence mounting that mindfulness reduces symptoms of ADHD. Teaching children to focus on one thing, as is done in meditation, yoga, visualization, and other mindfulness practices, appears to flex the focus center of the brain for other tasks.

The understanding of ADHD has evolved over the years from seeing it as a disorder of solely inattention and hyperactivity to seeing it as a disorder of executive functioning. Understanding ADHD and how it may affect your child's executive functioning is the first step in developing interventions. Be aware that there is no known "cure" for ADHD at this time, only management of the symptoms. Symptoms can lessen or change over time, and children can become high-functioning, successful adults with the proper support. In order to provide a strong foundation for success, parents of children with ADHD need to become educated consumers of interventions. In general, interventions include nutrition and exercise, medication, and behavioral modification. You should consult with your child's physician to determine the most appropriate intervention(s) for your child.

AUTISM SPECTRUM DISORDERS
Autism spectrum disorders (ASDs, sometimes called pervasive developmental disorders) include a variety of different conditions, such as autistic disorder (classic autism), Asperger's disorder, pervasive developmental disorder-not otherwise specified (PDD-NOS), Rett syndrome, and childhood disintegrative disorder (CDD). These disorders are considered on the autism "spectrum" because there is a wide variety of symptoms, skills,

and levels of impairment. Some children show very severe symptoms, while others show mild symptoms.

The core features of an ASD are impairments in socialization and communication, and repetitive or stereotyped behavior. Within each of these categories of impairment, there are executive functioning skills that can also be impaired.

Socialization

Children on the spectrum vary in their level of socialization, but all will show some degree of qualitative impairment. Some more severely impaired children will not show much social interest at all. There are other children who do not show interest but will reciprocate when caregivers or familiar people try to interact with them. There are also children on the spectrum who do appear to want social interaction, but they don't have the skills to be successful. They may have difficulties taking other people's points of view or be rigid in their thinking. The executive functioning skills required to be a good friend or have a positive relationship with caregivers and adults include both mental flexibility and emotional self-regulation.

Children with autism spectrum disorders may get upset when rules or plans are changed in the classroom. They may show rigidity in doing things "their way." They may also disengage and be in their own world, thereby missing instruction or opportunities to practice skills. Parents may seek support in building their child's social skills and executive functioning by collaborating with mental-health professionals and their child's school.

Communication

Some children with ASDs are completely nonverbal and others are extremely gifted in language (though they may show "pragmatic" language problems, such as difficulty waiting for their turn to speak, using proper greetings and goodbyes, looking at the speaker, and using nonverbal language, such as pointing, to indicate interest). Some children on the spectrum have a "little professor" style of communication, in which they espouse dictionary-like information to others on a topic of their own interest.

The executive functioning skills that may be lacking in children on the spectrum in relation to communication include flexibility (they may persist on a topic that interests them, regardless of the other person's level of interest) and emotional self-control (they may get upset when they are not allowed to talk about their interests).

Repetitive or Stereotyped Behaviors

Perhaps the most recognized feature of children with an autism spectrum disorder is repetitive or stereotyped behaviors (rocking, lining up objects, repeating the same phrase over and over), though some specialists argue that the difficulties with communication and socialization are actually the core features of the disorder. Some children have sensory sensitivities (difficulties with loud sounds or certain textures, showing unusual visual scrutiny of objects—looking at objects for a long time and in unusual ways, such as while tilting the head to the side or at a very close range.). Others will show repetitive motor movements, such as flapping hands, rocking, or hand-wringing. Yet others will show unusual preoccupation with parts of objects. For example, they may spin the wheels on a toy bus for hours.

Another feature that falls under this category is nonfunctional routines, which are routines that do not serve a purpose, and obsessions to maintain sameness. This lack of flexibility may be triggered unexpectedly, such as if a different route is taken to school or if there are changes in a school schedule. For example, a child with difficulties with changes in routine may have a meltdown if there is a schoolwide assembly that disrupts the normal day, or if math and reading times are switched, or if there is a substitute teacher.

In addition to the executive functioning skills of flexibility and emotional self-control, children on the autism spectrum also struggle with task initiation and task completion. For example, their rituals or repetitive motor movements can interfere with performing tasks, because they *must* finish their routine or movement. Additionally, difficulties with perspective-taking impede their ability to follow instructional comments. They may not understand that the teacher would like them to do something differently than how they are doing it, unless they are explicitly told. They struggle to infer and read social cues. Much of the reason children do the tasks their parents and teachers ask them to is because they want to please them, but children on the autism spectrum tend not to be particularly socially motivated to complete tasks for this reason.

LEARNING DISABILITIES

There are several different kinds of learning disabilities, though they all share common features. First, children and adolescents with learning disabilities usually have at least average to above-average intelligence. Second, they have below-average academic skills in at least one area (reading, writing, math) that is significantly lower than expected given their intelligence and school experience. This difference is sometimes referred to as a "significant discrepancy." Or they might not have a significant discrepancy, but they have had a lot of intervention in an academic area and they are making slower than expected progress. Lastly, they have a "processing deficit," which means there is one learning modality (e.g., visual, auditory, memory, speed, copying skills) that is below average.

Getting to the root of your child's executive functioning difficulties can be a long and frustrating process. You may see several professionals and still not get "The Answer." Since the developing mind is so complex, the assessment and interventions for your child may also be complex. As a conscious parent, you can take a step back and remind yourself that you are doing the best you can with the available information, and that this process is a step in the right direction to better understanding your child.

When a child has a learning disability, it is often difficult to sustain effort because her brain is working harder to process information than the brain of a child without a learning disability. If you think of a time when you had to do a cognitively taxing task and you were struggling, you might be able to understand how easy it is to give up or take frequent breaks. Children with learning disabilities also sometimes struggle with completing tasks in a timely manner, because of slower processing skills. For example, a child with a visual-motor processing deficit may fatigue easily on writing tasks. It would be a little like using your nondominant hand to write. You can do it, but it is harder, it takes longer, and your hand would likely get tired.

MEDICAL CONDITIONS

There are a variety of medical conditions that also contribute to executive functioning deficits. Conditions such as traumatic brain injuries, brain tumors, and seizure disorders all cause varying levels of executive functioning challenges. Children and adolescents who have undergone chemotherapy for cancer can also acquire such difficulties as a side effect of the treatment.

If your child has a medical condition, be sure to not only inform your child's school but also get a release-of-information form allowing your child's doctors to share information with your child's teacher and vice versa. This will help in coordinating interventions between your child's medical and school staff, and educating your child's teacher about the challenges that may present in his classroom.

Sleep disorders are also a major culprit in the development of executive functioning problems. Sleep apnea and sleep hypopnea are two such conditions that undermine quality sleep and can have substantial effects on functioning. Just think of a time when you were sleep-deprived—perhaps in the early months after having a baby, or when you were sick and had trouble sleeping—and how you were affected. Now imagine that you are chronically sleep-deprived, and you can see how you might have increased forgetfulness, difficulties concentrating, and other symptoms related to executive dysfunction. It is important to rule out sleep problems as a cause for executive functioning difficulties by consulting with medical professionals. Even if there is not a diagnosed sleep disorder, your child's doctor may be able to help you develop good sleep hygiene with your child so that she is getting the number of hours of sleep she needs.

EMOTIONAL DISORDERS

In the social-emotional realm, both anxiety and depression can cause impairments in executive functioning. In particular, children can show difficulties with activation energy and task initiation. A child with symptoms of depression may be lethargic or unmotivated to get going on tasks such as homework or chores. When children are depressed, they sometimes show tiredness as a symptom, and this makes it challenging to initiate activities, especially unappealing activities. They may even have a hard time doing things they enjoy, a symptom called anhedonia.

In the case of anxiety, you might observe that your child has a hard time starting something because she is too keyed up or on edge (a symptom called hyperarousal). Or, if a child is so anxious about performing well on a task, she might just avoid it altogether. You might see a child or adolescent procrastinating studying, for example, because then if she doesn't do well, she can blame it on not studying instead of not being smart. This protects her ego in case she doesn't do as well as she wants. A child or adolescent may also experience test anxiety, which is notorious for hijacking one's working memory. If you are focusing on your test worries, your brain is not free to focus on the content of the test you are taking.

Additionally, both anxiety and depression can cause severe difficulties in focus and concentration. Children can be internally distracted by their sadness or worries and have trouble paying attention to schoolwork as a result. It is important to consider emotional distraction as a potential cause of executive functioning problems. Consult with your child's doctor or a psychologist or psychiatrist for an assessment and recommendations for intervention.

Important Points to Consider

Conscious parenting is not a set of new rules you must follow, but rather a new lens for understanding your child's difficulties and responding to them in a way that nurtures your child and puts your relationship first.

○ There is no one "executive functioning disorder." There are executive functioning skills that may be more or less developed in your child at this point in time.

○ Every child develops differently, and being a conscious parent means you are aware, and not judging your child as "good" or "bad." Instead, think of his weaknesses as lagging skills that have yet to be taught.

○ There is a spectrum of development for executive functioning. Some children are "smooth sailors" and learn executive functioning skills with little instruction. Others are "boat rockers" in that they need more support to learn the same skills. Ask professionals who have experience with the range of development for information about where your child's development of executive functioning skills is in relation to same-age peers.

○ Before disciplining your child for not performing a task to the standard, ask yourself if it is a lack of will or a lack of skill. You may not be able to easily tell, but pause to consider the situation from your child's point of view. He may have the motivation to do well, but not the skill set. He may be just as disappointed and frustrated as you are. Empathize with his struggles.

○ As a conscious parent you are already aware of the importance of communication with your child. Keep an open dialogue with your child about how you can work together as a team to better understand and build his executive functioning skills.

 **CHAPTER 3**

The "Big Ten" Executive Functions

The executive functioning skills set is best thought of as an umbrella under which many different skills fall. These skills are all necessary for self-regulation, or being able to monitor, evaluate, and change one's behavior with a goal in mind. Take the time to think about your child and whether she has any of the challenges listed under each of the Big Ten executive functions. You can prioritize by the areas that create the most stress for you or your child, or the area that has the most challenges. The aim is not to focus on the negative traits, but to gain more information and be conscious and aware of her challenges. This lens helps you to focus on positive parenting practices that can support your child.

Task Initiation

Task initiation is the activation energy it takes to stop what you are currently doing and do something else. Children with executive functioning difficulties often have challenges stopping a preferred activity in order to do another, often nonpreferred, activity. In fact, even children (and adults!) without executive functioning difficulties may have these challenges. The difference between typical difficulties starting a new task and severe challenges is in the degree of difficulty in switching gears. A typical child may occasionally grumble and drag his feet about taking out the trash, or a teenager might sometimes put off studying until the last minute. A child or teenager with executive functioning problems chronically shows these behavior patterns. He may never get to his chores without a huge argument or multiple reminders, and he may be a chronic procrastinator such that he has severe sleep deprivation as a result of staying up late to finish things he should have started hours before. Children and adolescents with task initiation problems have to be torn away from things they are doing by others; they seem to lack the will power to do so themselves.

Ask yourself the following questions to determine the frequency of your child's difficulties with task initiation and check all that apply:

- ☐ Historically, has your child had a hard time beginning tasks independently?
- ☐ Does your child often say things like, "I don't know where to start!"?
- ☐ Does your child frequently need multiple reminders and prompts to get started on things?
- ☐ Does your child have a hard time stopping what he is doing to start something new?
- ☐ Would you describe your child as a "procrastinator"?
- ☐ Does your child frequently complain and delay when asked to do a nonpreferred activity?

If you checked three or more of these questions, your child likely has difficulties with task initiation, and you may want to target interventions in this area and see Chapter 4 for more information.

How do you know if your child has task initiation difficulties or is just lazy? Understand that difficulties with task initiation have many causes—difficulty understanding the task, challenges with knowing where to start, problems with visualizing the end product and planning how to get there, lagging skills in time awareness and management, etc. The process of switching gears to do something new is not automatic or seamless for children with executive functioning problems. Instead of thinking of difficulties getting starting on tasks as "laziness," think of them as lagging skills that need to be taught.

Response Inhibition

If you have ever talked yourself out of that delicious piece of cake, or have been successful in resisting the temptation to go online and check your Facebook page instead of writing a report for work, you have practiced response inhibition. Response inhibition is keeping yourself from acting impulsively, in order to achieve a goal. Young children often have great difficulties with delaying gratification because their time horizon is so short—they tend to think only of the here and now. But as children mature, their ability to control impulses improves, and they can think ahead to the consequences of acting impulsively. For example, they may forgo going to a baseball game with their friends because they have a paper due in a few days. They might turn off their phones to finish their homework if they know they have a lot of work to do. If friends call in the middle of their work, they will tell them that they will call them back when they're done. However, for children and adolescents with executive functioning difficulties, there is often a lag in the development of these response-inhibition skills.

Assess the degree to which your child shows response-inhibition challenges by checking the boxes next to the statements that apply:

☐ My child has always acted impulsively, from a very early age.

- [ ] My child tends to "jump first and think later," doing the first thing that comes to mind.
- [ ] It is very difficult for my child to think about and follow "if-then" contingencies (If I finish my chores now, then I can go play).
- [ ] I am constantly reminding my child to turn off screens (phones, computers, tablets, TV) when she is supposed to be working on homework.
- [ ] It is hard for my child to think about the consequences of her behavior.
- [ ] My child is impulsive in her work and makes careless mistakes.

If you checked three or more of these statements, your child likely has difficulties with response inhibition. You may wish to target this area for intervention and read Chapter 5 for more helpful advice.

Focus

In order to learn or practice skills, children must learn how to focus their attention. Paying attention involves directing your attention to what you are supposed to be doing, keeping that focus long enough to finish your task, and all the while filtering out distractions. Children and adolescents with executive functioning difficulties can have challenges with any or all of these processes. Distractibility comes in many forms as well. Some children are internally distracted, and they spend their time daydreaming or thinking of other things. Others are externally distracted, and they will direct their attention to anything in their environment—noises, people, objects, you name it. When a child has problems with focus, it can be during listening, and he can miss important instructions or information. Or you may see focus problems when it comes to your child sitting down and completing homework without getting sidetracked. Needless to say, helping a child who is easily distracted can wear on even the most patient of parents. And yet, teaching focus and strategies for managing distraction is one of the most powerful gifts you can give your child, because it can help with many different areas in his life.

Using the following checklist, you can assess the degree to which your child is showing focus difficulties:

- ☐ Does it seem as if your child is not hearing you when you give directions?
- ☐ Does your child have difficulties sticking with one task, especially if it requires patience and concentration?
- ☐ Do you find your child paying attention to background noises when he is doing homework?
- ☐ Does your child have a hard time staying on topic when talking?
- ☐ Does your child complain that it is hard to concentrate?
- ☐ Do your child's teachers report to you that he has a hard time focusing in the classroom?

If you checked three or more as true for your child, you will likely be looking for interventions to help strengthen your child's focusing skills. You can also see Chapter 6 for more on helping your child focus.

Children with focus issues often have self-esteem issues as well. This is because they receive so much corrective feedback ("Pay attention!" "You forgot this part!" "What did I say?"). Even if the feedback is neutral or constructive, it is still someone telling them they aren't doing something correctly. Balance this out by giving positive feedback as well ("I like how you checked your work!" "Great job following my directions!").

Time Management

Even adults struggle with completing all the tasks they need to do within a finite amount of time. Is it any surprise that children with executive functioning difficulties, who have trouble setting goals, forecasting the future, and being aware of passing time, also have difficulties with time management?

The challenges only seem to increase for adolescents, who have more responsibilities, afterschool activities, and desires for peer interaction. The battle between tasks on the "have to do" list and tasks on the "want to do" list can create procrastination and avoidance behavior. Children and adolescents with time-management issues may be chronically late, lose track of time, overestimate what they can accomplish in a period of time, or rush through things to finish on time. The good news is that time management is a learned skill, and therefore can be taught to children and teens.

Referencing the following checklist, you can determine if your child struggles with time-management tasks:

- ☐ Does your child often lose track of time?
- ☐ Does your child underestimate how much time a task will take?
- ☐ Does your child set unrealistic goals for how much she can complete in a time period?
- ☐ Without your reminders, would your child forget appointments or scheduled activities?
- ☐ Does your child complain that she runs out of time on tests at school?
- ☐ Does your child seem unaware of passing time?

If you checked three or more of these items, you may want to prioritize developing interventions for time management for your child. See Chapter 7 for more on time management.

Working Memory

Working memory is the process of holding information in your mind long enough to do something with it (remember it, process it, act on it). Think of it as RAM (random access memory) in the computer of your brain: It determines how much you can have on your hard drive without crashing. Working memory is especially important for learning—you must be able to remember what is said in the short term in order to learn it for the long term. Children and adolescents with working memory challenges often miss parts of conversations, instructions, and lectures and as a result have pieces of the learning puzzle missing. They may also seem forgetful and lose track of what they are doing midstream.

Using the checklist that follows, identify which statements are true for your child:

☐ My child has difficulties following directions with more than one part.
☐ My child has to frequently reread what he has read to understand.
☐ My child forgets to write things down (for example, what he has for homework).
☐ My child has a hard time with mental math.
☐ My child has difficulties doing more than one task at a time.

If you checked three or more of these items as true for your child, you may wish to target working memory as an area for improvement and read Chapter 8 for more helpful tips.

Working memory can be improved. Studies have shown that exercise is one of the best ways to improve working memory because of the increased blood flow to the brain.

Flexibility

Flexibility as an executive function is the process of being able to shift your ideas and plans in changing conditions. Children who struggle with mental flexibility (sometimes referred to as cognitive flexibility) often get "stuck" on one way to solve a problem, or get fixated on an inefficient strategy. They may also focus in on a detail of a problem and lose the big picture. Mental flexibility is important for academic problem-solving. Academically, children with difficulties with cognitive flexibility tend to learn by a rote strategy—memorizing through repetition. However, as curricula become more complex, children are expected to learn by abstraction—taking what they know and applying it to a new learning situation. Without flexibility, children tend to have difficulty when a problem is slightly different than what they learned, or if they are asked to synthesize what they know to solve a new problem.

Mental flexibility is also essential in social problem-solving. Social rules are always changing depending on the situation. For example, the volume of your voice changes when you are in class and when you are on the playground. Your level of chattiness and self-disclosure depends on whom you are talking to and where you are. You have to read social cues in "real time" to see if someone is no longer interested in what you are saying, or if you've offended him by what you've said. You need flexibility to adapt to changing social situations. Especially when children get older, there are more "unwritten" rules. Kids no longer say, "I don't want to play with you" directly; instead they may make excuses or avoid you, or even be nice to you in person but then talk negatively about you when you are not there. These types of social situations can be complicated for a child or teen with executive functioning challenges in mental flexibility to understand and adapt to.

Children on the autism spectrum often have difficulties with cognitive flexibility in social problem-solving. Research shows that one potential cause is that they often do not engage in "self-talk." While typical children will talk through their problem-solving ideas in their head, children on the spectrum may not. However, the good news is that teaching children to talk through ideas has been shown to improve cognitive flexibility.

So how do you know if your child struggles with cognitive flexibility? Using the following checklist, mark which behaviors you have observed in your child:

- ☐ My child gets "stuck" on one way of solving a problem.
- ☐ My child sometimes insists that her way of doing schoolwork is best, even though it is an ineffective strategy.

☐ My child can be a "black and white" thinker, and miss the shades of gray in problem-solving.

☐ My child has trouble adapting to new social situations and understanding unwritten social rules.

☐ My child sometimes seems to have a "my way or the highway" mentality when interacting with other children.

If you checked three or more of these challenges in cognitive flexibility, you may wish to choose this as an area to begin interventions. See Chapter 9 for more information on flexibility and your child.

Self-Regulation

Self-regulation is being able to reflect on your actions and behaviors and make needed changes to reach a goal. Becoming a self-regulated learner is a complex process that involves several ongoing phases. Students with strong self-regulation skills engage in a process called metacognition, which is thinking about their thinking; that is, they actively contemplate the learning process. They set goals, make a plan, execute the plan, monitor how the plan is going, make adjustments if it is not going well, observe their performance and take mental notes about what is working and what is not, and, after competing the task, evaluate and self-reflect on their performance. These skills are developmental in nature, meaning that we do not expect the young child to go through all these steps consciously. However, the seeds of self-regulation in academics are planted as early as infancy and toddlerhood. Parents and teachers can model and teach self-regulation skills.

Take for example the process required to do a word problem. A child with deficits in self-regulation may look at the problem and just jump in by taking the numbers he sees in the problem and adding them up or subtracting them, without much thought. A child with strong self-regulation might read the problem a few times, make a drawing about what the problem is asking, search for key words in the problem that give clues about which operation to use, set up and compute the problem, and then ask herself, "Does my answer make sense?" She might talk through all of these steps out loud or in her mind to help her stay on track. On a larger scale, a self-regulated learner might make a study plan for an upcoming math test on word problems. He might imagine himself studying at home with his dad and asking his teacher for help if he gets stuck, all in advance of actually studying. He might decide to do practice problems because that has worked for him in the past. He would likely study a little at a time and not all at once the morning of the test. Throughout the process, he would be constantly asking himself, "Do I understand this?" and reflecting on his level of understanding. A student with poor self-regulation skills might not have a mental image of what it "looks like" to study. He might look at the problems the night before and not be aware if he understands them, and thus wouldn't take steps to ensure he did before the test.

Does your child struggle with self-regulated learning? Does he struggle with thinking about what he needs to do? Children with self-regulation issues often fail to consistently think through, evaluate, and change their approaches to learning, even when they have been explicitly taught to do so. Think about whether your child engages in any of the following behaviors to determine if self-regulation is an area of challenge to target for intervention:

- ☐ My child does not seem to set goals for himself when it comes to academics.
- ☐ My child has trouble knowing when he doesn't understand a learning task.
- ☐ My child doesn't seem to know his strengths and weaknesses as a learner.
- ☐ My child rarely makes a plan for studying for a test or a long-term project.
- ☐ My child makes frequent mistakes in his work but doesn't seem to notice.
- ☐ My child doesn't ask for help with his work as much as he should.

If you checked three or more behaviors as problematic for your child, you may consider intervention for developing self-regulation strategies. You can find more information on self-regulation in Chapter 10.

Emotional Self-Control

Emotional self-control is the process of managing your emotions and reflecting on your feelings in order to keep yourself from engaging in impulsive behaviors. The skills required for emotional self-control include awareness of feelings, using verbal labels for feelings (sad, frustrated, irritated, excited), and controlling responses to situations without acting impulsively. When children have difficulties controlling their emotions, they often engage in negative behaviors, such as hitting, impulsively saying inappropriate or unkind things, or committing other forms of aggression. Not all children act out when their emotions get the better of them. Some children turn inward and have worried thoughts or sadness and have a hard time letting go of hurt feelings.

Of course, your child's ability to regulate her feelings greatly depends on age. Any parent who has witnessed a toddler throw a tantrum can attest that young children struggle with emotional self-control! At the same time, a sulking teenager can be struggling with emotional self-control in a different way. No matter what age your child is, as a parent, you can coach your child to manage her feelings and engage in appropriate emotional self-control. There is good reason to do so; children with more self-control do better in school. This is because in school, children are expected to manage their frustration with academic tasks, cooperate and problem-solve peer conflicts so as to not disrupt learning, and navigate the multiple expectations that are placed on them without acting out or shutting down.

While all children struggle with processing and expressing emotions at some point in their development, children with executive functioning challenges may have amplified challenges in the area of emotional self-control. Using the following checklist, indicate the statements that are true for your child, in order to gauge if emotional self-control is an area to target for intervention:

☐ I would describe my child as a highly emotional individual.
☐ My child's moods change very quickly.
☐ My child has always been difficult to soothe when upset.
☐ My child is quick to disagree or argue with adults and peers.

☐ When corrected, my child has strong emotional reactions.
☐ My child's behavior is out of control.
☐ My child gets into "funks" and it is hard for her to get out of them.

If you checked three or more of these statements as true for your child, you might want to consider targeting emotional self-control as an area for intervention and reading Chapter 11 for further advice.

Task Completion

Task completion is the process of sustaining your levels of attention and energy to see a task to the end. Difficulties completing tasks can occur at home and at school. At home, you might notice that chores are partially done, or not done to the standard. You may find that your child needs a lot of extra prompting to finish tasks that he has started. Sometimes the last phase of an activity—cleaning up—is left undone. Children with executive functioning challenges often have trouble seeing tasks to the end, even enjoyable tasks, projects, and hobbies.

If your child has difficulties with task completion, you might hear his teacher describe his behavior as "off-task." Ask the teacher what your child is doing when he is off-task in order to better understand his challenges. Also, ask the teacher during which assignments or subjects or times of day he is off-task or on-task to get clues as to the underlying cause of the difficulty with task completion.

One of the main domains where you might see these challenges is in the area of homework completion. Completing homework requires an internal stick-to-itiveness. Some children show a lag in developing this persistence. The reasons for children not seeing homework tasks to the end are complex. It is often more than a pure motivation issue. Sometimes children don't understand the task, or are overwhelmed and don't know where to start. Sometimes they can get started but when they get stuck, they shut down and avoid the task. There is often avoidance and expression of dislike for the task when the task is too hard and the child does not want to admit it or ask for help. On the flip side, sometimes the tasks are too easy and are boring for the child. To help uncover the roots of your child's difficulties with homework completion, you will likely need to engage in collaboration with your child's teacher(s) in addition to tackling the problem at home.

Is task completion a problem for your child? Use this checklist to identify areas that may pose a challenge for your child by checking those statements that apply:

- ☐ My child is off-task when doing chores, resulting in them being partially done or taking a long time to be done.
- ☐ My child needs a lot of reminders and prompts to see homework to the end.
- ☐ If I don't sit next to my child while he is doing homework, it won't get finished.
- ☐ My child seems to only put effort into things he likes to do.
- ☐ Teachers frequently tell me that my child doesn't finish his work in the classroom.
- ☐ My child gives up easily when doing homework.
- ☐ My child doesn't finish tasks or projects, even if they are enjoyable.

If you checked three or more of these as problematic for your child, task completion may be an area on which you will want to focus your interventions. See Chapter 12 for more information on task completion.

Organization

Organization is the process of keeping track and taking care of your belongings (personal belongings, schoolwork) and maintaining order in your personal space. Children with executive functioning weaknesses frequently have difficulties with organization. Their rooms are often messy, their backpacks full of crumpled papers, their desks full of random things, their notebooks disorganized, and they are "frequent flyers" to the lost-and-found at their schools! They often forget to turn in their work because they left it at home or in the car, or cannot find it in their messy backpacks when they need it.

Children with organizational challenges are often frustrating to parents and teachers because they don't understand why they just can't get it together. It is important to think of the frustration that these children are experiencing as well. Often, despite motivation and best intentions, they fall short of adult expectations. They can then feel disappointed in themselves. At times, adults can jump in and try to organize for the child, which helps in the short run, but it doesn't really teach the child the skills she needs to be self-sufficient in organization.

To what degree does your child show organizational impairments? Use the following checklist to pinpoint areas of challenge:

- ☐ My child seems to create messes wherever she goes.
- ☐ My child is constantly losing belongings, such as jackets, lunch-boxes, homework, books, and important papers.
- ☐ My child doesn't seem to know where to put things, even after I explain where things should go.
- ☐ My child's notebooks are not organized by subject; they seem to have papers from all subjects randomly placed in them with no order.
- ☐ My child frequently fails to bring the right books, papers, or notebooks home with her.
- ☐ I frequently get calls or texts from my child asking me to bring something to school that she forgot.
- ☐ My child's workspace is messy and disorganized.

If you checked three or more areas as problematic for your child, then you may want to prioritize teaching your child organizational strategies. Read more on organizational strategies in Chapter 13.

Prioritizing Interventions

When you have a child with many different types of executive functioning challenges, it can be hard to decide where to start with intervention. Hopefully this chapter provided you with a structure for understanding what the Big Ten executive functions might look like for your child at home and at school. From these descriptions and the checklists, you might have been able to pinpoint some areas you can start targeting for intervention. You might have been able to see that your child has some executive functioning strengths as well.

So how do you prioritize which area of executive functioning should be tackled first? In order to set up a game plan for deciding which area to target for intervention, you might ask yourself a few questions:

- Which area of executive functioning creates the most difficulty for my child?

- Which area creates the most disruption in our family life?

- Which area causes the most difficulty at school?

After answering these questions, you may have between one and three different areas in which you want your child to improve. From here, you can take one of two approaches: start with the area that you think will be the easiest to work on, or start with the one that causes the most disruption in the life of your child. If you choose the latter, be sure to start with small, achievable goals so he does not get overwhelmed.

Important Points to Consider

A key component of being a conscious parent is to better understand the motivation behind your child's behavior. Looking at the Big Ten executive functions and asking yourself which are areas of strength and weakness is a step in the right direction toward understanding why your child acts the way she does.

○ Respect where your child is in her development at this point in time. Set an intention to be present-minded instead of wishing she was further along in her skills.

○ Use self-talk such as "Right now, she is doing the best she can with the skills she has" when you experience negative emotions because your child is not demonstrating the behavior you would like in the moment.

○ Keep the lines of communication open and positive with your child about your intentions. Let her know that you are working on ways to help her learn and improve her skills and you will need her feedback on what is working and not working. Validating your child's point of view and listening fully to her concerns will help the collaborative process of learning new strategies.

 **CHAPTER 4**

Task Initiation: Taming Your Child's Procrastination Monster

Starting on a task is often half the battle in getting something done. Children and adolescents with executive functioning challenges frequently have difficulty with initiation. They might procrastinate, drag their feet, or be so overwhelmed they don't know how to begin. You might think of these children as locomotive trains trying to get up a big hill—it takes them a long time to get moving, but once they do, they can often chug along smoothly. This "activation energy" is key for task initiation, and parents can learn strategies for helping their "locomotives" get their engines running! The first step in helping is to understand the root of your child's difficulties in starting tasks. By understanding the causes, you are less likely to respond in annoyance, anger, or frustration when your child seems to be taking forever to do a task.

What Is Task Initiation?

Beginning a task such as homework or chores or even following a direction is more complex than you might guess at first glance. Adults seamlessly go through a process to start a task without even thinking about it. What you actually do when you start a task is think about the task, imagine yourself doing the task, imagine what it might feel like to start and finish the task, motivate yourself to complete the task, anticipate what would happen if you did not do the task, mentally plan the steps in the task, think about when the best time would be to do the task, pause in the task you are already doing, gather the needed materials, and then begin the task.

Children and adolescents often need explicit coaching on these steps, particularly if they have executive functioning deficits. You may wonder why your child can't just focus on the task and be done with it! The reason is that some children require more external cues, such as parents and teachers talking them through the task or modeling how to do the task, than others. Some children and adolescents also struggle with anticipating the positive consequences of doing the task or the negative consequences of not doing the task. These are children who continually receive negative consequences for not starting (and thus, not finishing) a task, and yet they continue to put off tasks over and over again. In adolescence, this can often take the form of extreme procrastination. To support your child, you need to understand that the level of intervention required to facilitate completion of a task varies by age and developmental level.

The Young Child (Ages 1–4)

When you think of a toddler or preschooler, it may seem silly to think that you can teach executive functioning skills to him! Toddlers are very "in the moment" and do not have the ability to think and plan far into the future. Their language is also limited, so they cannot talk themselves through complex tasks. Can you imagine a toddler saying, "I think I'm going to get my sweater just in case it gets chilly at the park later," or "I don't feel like putting away my dishes right now, but I will do it because when I am done I can have free play time"? However, there are things parents can do to lay the foundation for self-regulation and the development of executive functioning. In particular, there are a number of ways to support task-initiation skills.

TRANSITION PROMPTS

One of the first things that a toddler must learn to do in order to complete a task or follow a direction is to stop what he is already doing. This transition can be the most challenging part of starting a new task. For example, if it is time to take a bath, and the toddler is busy playing with toys, he must stop playing, perhaps put away the toys, and go into the bathroom to get in the tub. Anyone who has ever tried to abruptly pick up a toddler who is busy having fun with his toys knows that it doesn't always go well! Think about it: What if you were having a great time talking to a friend and someone swooped in and made you go take a bath without warning? You might be pretty upset too. There are a number of ways to support transitions to new tasks.

First, give your child a verbal "heads-up" that he is going to be expected to stop what he is doing. This might be something like "In two minutes, it will be time to put away your toys and take a bath." Then, right before the transition, give another prompt: "Okay, two minutes is up. Time for your bath." If this is sufficient, congratulations! If you are met with a protest, you can verbally mediate what might be going through your child's mind and present the new task as something that may be enjoyable: "I know it is hard to stop playing when you are having fun, but we can continue playing in the tub now!"

Since young children do not have a strong sense of time, you can also provide a visual aid to show how long before a transition. For example, you can set the timer on your phone or set a kitchen timer and let your child know that when the timer goes off it is time to transition.

Sometimes transitions can be facilitated by music or song. It's no coincidence that in most preschools, music is played when it is time to clean up, or the class sings a clean-up song. This is because music is a great cue for transitions. You can borrow a clean-up song from a TV show, children's music, or your child's preschool, or make up your own. Sing the same song for all cleaning-up situations and the child will learn that this always means that he is about to change activities. It makes it a bit more fun for the child. You still may be met with protest, but be consistent and your child will learn.

MODELING TRANSITION LANGUAGE

Even before young children can speak, they are processing and understanding language. Studies have shown that even as young as six months old, babies know what you are saying. So when you talk out loud about transitions, children are building an understanding of the unspoken thoughts that adults go through when they are about to start a new task. This is invaluable practice for when they will be starting tasks on their own.

Did you know that even before children can speak, they can understand and remember transitions? They have what is called "nonverbal working memory," which is a picture in their mind of what happens before and after a transition. They don't have the words to tell you, but they are remembering sequences of events.

One of the first language concepts that toddlers must develop to understand transitions is "first-then." It might sound something like "First we play with toys, then we take a bath," or in even simpler language, "First shirt, then pants." You can say these first-then statements for all kinds of tasks, and it will help build an understanding of sequencing. Using first-then statements in general will then support kids' understanding that sometimes they have to do a nonpreferred task (put away dishes, eat vegetables) before they get to do a preferred task (play with toys, eat dessert). As kids get older, you can introduce "first-next-then" statements to build an understanding of three-step directions. You can say the statement, then as you do each step, emphasize the transition word. For example, "*First*, we put away our toys, *next* we get our bath toys, *then* we take a bath. Okay, *first*, we put away our toys . . ."

Another language concept to model out loud is "before" and "after." This is done in much the same way first-then is modeled. It is a slightly trickier concept to learn, though, so you should try to introduce it early and practice it often. This is a big concept for when kids enter school, because teachers use it all the time ("Before lunch we are going to do a spelling test" or "After we do our math workbook it is time for free play."). Use "before" and "after" to talk about time during the day. For example, if a toddler asks, "Where's Daddy?" you could say, "He will be home *after* your nap." Then reinforce the concept by pointing it out when the event happens ("See? Daddy is home. Remember I said he'd be home *after* your nap? Here he is!").

Some children have difficulties with understanding and producing language. Children with speech and language difficulties may need additional intervention to understand and use first-then, before and after, and other language concepts. Consult with a speech and language pathologist if you have concerns about your child's ability to understand and use language.

VISUAL SUPPORT

Because young children's language is still developing, they may need visual support to better understand transitions. Children with executive functioning challenges may be lacking in their ability to visualize what it looks like to start a task and thus may not know where to start. It would be like someone asking you to put together a puzzle without looking at the picture on the box. It can be done, but it's a lot easier if you know what the final puzzle looks like.

So how do you give your child visual support for starting a task? There are a number of ways, and the level of intervention will vary by how severe the child's executive functioning challenges are. Some parents find that simply gesturing toward the new task, such as pointing to the bathtub, will suffice. Others find that they need to show a child a picture of the transition. This can be a picture from a book or Google Images, or a drawing. In general, photographs are somewhat better than drawings, but either will do. If the child really needs support in transitioning, you can take a photograph of the child doing the task another time and print it out for reference. So, for example, take pictures of your child playing, cleaning up, and taking a bath. Then print them out, put them in sequence, and show them to your child as you give the direction. You can also purchase a wall hanger from a teacher supply store that has clear pockets in it for visual schedules. Or if you are crafty, you can make your own by putting Velcro or magnets on the back of each photograph and sticking them to either a wall or your fridge. You can do either a vertical or horizontal array, but the sequence should be top-to-bottom or left-to-right. Then, when it is time for the transition, you can put the photographs in the correct order and show the child what the sequence of events will be.

REINFORCEMENT

It goes without saying that young children need positive feedback. Some children are socially motivated and a "Good job!" or "I'm proud of you!" will be enough. In terms of praise, it also helps to be specific about what the child did a good job on and what you are proud of ("Good job putting away your toys when Mom asked you to!" or "I'm proud of you for following directions to get your bath toys!"). The praise can also be incremental. If your child partially does the task, go ahead and praise the effort, because it will build persistence for the next time ("I like how you put away your blocks. I'll help with the trains this time.").

Some children require tangible rewards to understand the connection between doing the desired behavior and getting parental approval. Or they understand the connection, but they are more motivated to make an effort if it will earn them a sticker or a reward. There are many different ways to set up a positive-reinforcement plan for children. The basic premise is the same, though: Define the behavior you want, remind the child of the incentive ("When you are done you will get a sticker/choice of book/special snack"), and after the behavior is done, provide the reward *as soon as possible.* Young children are very "in the now," so if there is a big time delay they will not understand that they got the reward because they did the desired behavior. They may even make a wrong connection because they did something in between the desired behavior and the reward. For example, if your child took his bath, and ten minutes later threw a tantrum because you asked him to brush his teeth, then you gave him a sticker for the bath, he could think the sticker was for the tantrum and not the bath.

It may be tempting to take away stickers for other negative behaviors that may come up. This is not recommended, because the stickers should represent one thing: if I do X behavior, I get my sticker. Think of other consequences for misbehavior. Your child should be playing to win, not playing to not lose.

Also, if you are giving stickers that can be redeemed for rewards (for example, ten stickers get the child a special treat), be sure that the bar is low enough in the beginning that he gets a taste of success. You can always raise the bar as he becomes successful, but if the bar is initially set too high, then he may give up.

The Elementary-Age Child (Ages 5–12)

Once children are school-age, the demands on their ability to start tasks increase with each grade. The level of independence also increases. Children in kindergarten through second grade tend to have much more guidance to get started on tasks, and then in third through fifth grade, the teachers begin to decrease their support in an effort to build independent-learning skills. Children are expected to start on their work right away, and even anticipate what they should start working on in advance of the teacher telling them what to do. Children with executive functioning weakness tend to struggle more with each passing year, and continue to require more support than their peers in learning how to start tasks. Parents may also notice that it is difficult to get their child to begin homework, and see an increase in the child putting off tasks until the last minute.

THE PREMACK PRINCIPLE

The Premack Principle is a social-psychology theory that suggests that people are motivated to complete an undesirable task in order to do a desired task. For example, if a child loves watching TV, her parents might make a rule that she must put away her dishes from dinner before she can watch TV. By this theory, this makes cleaning dishes more likely to happen because a reward follows. Just as a young child is learning first-then sequences, the elementary-age child is learning that if she gets something she doesn't like to do done, it will free up her time to do what she wants to do.

Unfortunately, many children with executive functioning challenges do not naturally follow the Premack Principle. They may argue against the rule, do the desired behavior anyway, or complain that the rule is unfair and have an emotional reaction or act out. This is in part because some children have a hard time imaging the positive feeling of the future when they will get to do what they want; instead they focus on the negative feeling of doing the unpleasant task. Parents can help by asking them to picture what it will look like when they are finished ("I will be relaxed on the couch with my favorite show, and my parents will be smiling"). They can also ask the child what it will feel like to be done with the task ("I will feel proud that I got it out of the way, and I will feel relaxed that I am free to watch TV"). It may also help to acknowledge the negative feeling ("I know you don't feel like starting your math homework") and provide encouragement and support ("I will help you get started so you can go outside and play when you are done.").

Ensure that your child knows how to do the task before assuming it is a task-initiation problem. Break down a larger task that you know he cannot do independently into smaller steps he can do. You may need to first show your child how to do the small steps and then give him a chance to practice each step.

THE POWER OF CHOICE

If there are several tasks to begin, a child may not know where to start. For example, when given homework in a few different subjects, the child may start with the easiest work, or do the hardest work first, or avoid starting altogether. You can help your child by first evaluating the task difficulty of each assignment and making a plan together. Your child could rate how hard something might be by sorting the work into "easy," "medium," or "hard," or by rating each assignment on a ten-point scale, with one being very easy and ten being very hard. She can then choose whether she wants to get the hard work out of the way or finish the easy work first for a quicker start. This process will help her understand which system works best for her. It also enables her to have a sense of power over her homework, because she gets to make the choice about what to do. She may not have a choice about whether or not she has homework, but a little bit of choice can be motivating.

Kids who are given choices about task sequences (in what order they can do their work) demonstrate higher percentages of time on-task, task completion, and accuracy.

TEACHING GOAL-SETTING

Children in elementary school are beginning to be able to plan ahead a day or two and thus can set goals ("I need to finish my book report tonight because it is due in two days and tomorrow I have soccer all evening"). They are also learning to remember a weekly schedule ("I have soccer on Tuesdays"). Of course, children will also likely still need reminders and parental support to think ahead. One of the ways to help children initiate a task, such as a book report, is to help them set a goal for completing it. Some children will try to put off a project or studying because it is not due the next day.

Having a family calendar posted with icons (picture of a soccer ball, an icon for a test or due date) may help your child remember a schedule and make plans to finish projects. She can visualize how far away a due date is and make a goal for what she wants to complete each night before it is due.

After the due date, circle back and discuss the successful strategy used ("I'm glad you did your rough draft this weekend because it was much less stressful finishing your report the day before it was due."). This feedback loop will help children "file away" successful experiences in starting tasks on time instead of procrastinating.

> Goal-setting is a core feature of executive functioning. It helps children and adolescents think ahead and begin evaluating whether they achieve their goals. The process of planning and reflecting is essential for building independence.

BUILDING A HOMEWORK ROUTINE

Starting on homework tasks is easier if you have a routine. If the routine is established early on in your child's school career, it will be helpful when she gets older and has to initiate and monitor her own routine later on. The first step in building a homework routine is to designate a space for homework. This space should be free from technology and screens (TV, Internet, phones) and have plenty of space and good lighting. The next step is to designate a time for homework. Is it right when the child gets home? Is it after a snack and a little "downtime"? Is it after dinner? After a sport? Some kids need a break when they get home, just as adults need a break after a full day of work. Other kids can't handle taking a break because they have a hard time revving back up for school tasks once they relax. Each family will have to experiment and find the time that is the most productive.

The key is being consistent in the routine once it is established. Children who know there is a set homework routine will be less likely to fight it, because it becomes an expectation. If you sometimes let the TV be on, and sometimes not, you will get kids asking for it to be on again and again.

The Adolescent (Ages 13–18+)

Teenagers may begin to present unique challenges when it comes to task-initiation difficulties, because they are starting to desire more independence and can resent parental monitoring. This becomes a double bind when you have an adolescent with executive functioning difficulties; he may not be ready for independence because of lagging skills in planning, organizing, and following through.

THE EVENING ROUTINE

As with the elementary-age child, it is important to build a consistent evening routine for completing chores and homework. However, this can sometimes be more challenging with adolescents, because they often have more activities, sports, and school subjects to juggle. The adolescent may end up having to work on homework late at night, and some adolescents even claim that they can't work until late at night. They might procrastinate so that they feel the pressure and can force themselves to work.

According to the National Sleep Foundation, adolescents need about 9¼ hours of sleep each night to function best (for some, 8½ hours is enough). Most teens do not get enough sleep—one study found that only 15 percent reported sleeping 8½ hours on school nights.

To compound the problem, adolescents tend to have shifts in their sleep patterns, in which they don't get tired until later at night. This "sleep drift" creates a lack of sleep, especially if they procrastinate and stay up late finishing assignments and have to get up early the next day for school. This is why it is essential to teach your adolescent an evening routine and good sleep hygiene. If your teen has difficulties with task initiation, chances are addressing this problem will help with sleep problems, as he will be able to go to bed earlier.

PROCRASTINATION MONSTERS

Is your teenager a procrastinator? Does he put things off until the very last minute? Does he claim he can't work unless he is under pressure? Could something that takes thirty minutes end up taking hours? These are all signs of a lurking "procrastination monster." This monster eats up your teenager's time and feeds on stress. Teaching your teenager how to combat this monster will be one of the most important tools you can give him to be a successful student.

One technique for curbing procrastination is to teach your teenager why it is so powerful. The reason people get stuck in a cycle of procrastination is that it is very reinforcing. Why? Because if you put something off (such as studying for a test) and then you do well, you can say to yourself, "Hey, I'm smart! I barely studied and I did well!" And if you end up doing poorly, you can say to yourself, "Well, it's because I didn't study until the last minute." Either way, you protect your ego. So, in a way, there is no immediate consequence for procrastination (except when you get a poor grade, but then you can explain it away as lack of effort). Once teenagers know why procrastination is so powerful, they may begin to think about why they do it. Might it be a way to protect themselves from feeling bad if they don't do well? If so, then learning to take risks is the intervention.

It can sometimes be difficult to watch your adolescent put off tasks until the last minute, and then deal with a grouchy sleep-deprived teen in the morning. Acknowledge your own feelings (disappointed, annoyed, angry, concerned) but do not dwell on the incident or act on it in that moment. Instead, try to empathize with your teen's challenges and have a conversation with her later when you are no longer upset ("I feel concerned when you don't get enough sleep because it affects both your mood and the family harmony in the morning. Can we problem-solve how to get you started on your homework earlier so you can get good sleep?").

Another strategy for teaching teenagers to combat procrastination is to teach them tricks for starting tasks they don't want to do. This can be done by taking something big and making it smaller. For example, if you tell yourself, "I'll never finish this essay; it's too long" or "I don't want to do this essay because it's too hard" or "These math problems are so boring," chances are you won't start on these tasks. If you take the big statement and shrink it to something manageable, the likelihood of you starting (and finishing) is much higher. So you could tell yourself, "This essay may be long, but I can just start with a thesis statement" or "This essay seems hard, but I can start with an outline and see how it goes" or "This math isn't very exciting, but I can work for ten minutes and then take a break." Chances are, once they get started, it is often not as difficult, long, or boring as they thought. And even if it is, they will have made some progress toward completion and that can be motivation to keep going.

Procrastination is also fueled by distractions. In a world of exciting interactions at the tip of adolescents' fingers—their entire social network, the latest celebrity gossip, all of their favorite shows just a download away—it's no wonder they put off something mundane like homework. There are teenagers who report that they *prefer* distractions because it breaks up the monotony of homework. The problem is that the research shows that these distractions impair learning and memory. Teaching your child to use technology as a reward or a break is key for developing successful study routines. Talk with your teenager about when he tends to break away from studying to procrastinate—during hard tasks? When he gets stuck? When he gets bored? Having your teenager reflect on the triggers for procrastination behavior is the start of developing an intervention for combatting it.

RECOGNIZING FAILURE-AVOIDANT TRAPS

In addition to procrastination, there are a number of other self-handicapping thoughts and behaviors that can interfere with task initiation. Some students base their self-worth on their academic performance alone. If such a student also has executive functioning challenges, he can become hopeless about his ability to change his negative pattern of behavior. For example, a student who habitually puts in low effort and doesn't start assignments until the last minute may be doing so partially because he can blame the low effort if he doesn't do well. Some other students may even diminish their success as "luck" and not take credit for their achievements. Parents can help students with these feelings understand the paths to success by emphasizing the values of effort, persistence, proactivity, seeking support, and building a tolerance for failure.

Parents play a strong role in encouraging students to change their patterns of behavior. Start by acknowledging your child's feelings and then offer to help brainstorm possible solutions. Let her know that everyone struggles from time to time with getting started on tasks. Normalizing the process may make her feel better about seeking help.

VISUALIZATION

Adolescents can seem unmotivated to start tasks, particularly if they also have executive functioning difficulties, because they may not know where to start. People tend to think of internal motivation for school as a personality trait when it actually is a situational trait. Thinking about motivation as a situational trait may help adolescents start on tasks they perceive as undesirable. Just as with adults, there are times when adolescents are more motivated than others, depending on a number of factors, including the type of task, whether it is perceived as an interesting or useful task, if there is a positive relationship between the adolescent and the person asking him to do the task, if there are competing tasks that are more engaging, if the task is difficult, and so on.

Help your child identify the times when he is motivated to show him that he is not an "unmotivated" student; rather, there are times when he is motivated and times when he is not. This will prevent patterns of defeatist thinking ("I'm lazy and unmotivated, so there's nothing I can do about it") and encourage patterns of thinking that support task initiation ("I am eager to do math because I am good at it, but I will need some more support in writing this essay because it's not my favorite thing to do.").

Some adolescents with executive functioning problems do not automatically visualize a positive emotion of the future, a time when they are finished with the task. Instead, they get stuck on the present negative emotion. Visualization of positive emotions of the future can be motivating to start on tasks. For example, you could guide your adolescent to think of what it will look and feel like when he is all finished with his work ("I am on my bed, chatting with friends, without having to worry about doing any work" or "I am turning in my work and getting a smile from the teacher for turning it in on time."). This visualization can sometimes be a catalyst to getting started.

Social Media and Procrastination

Social media outlets can create problems for adolescents who have a hard time starting on tasks. Why? Because they are so reinforcing! Teenagers have access to all their friends and their social world on their phones and computers. There are alerts telling you when someone new is online, when someone likes something you said, or when someone wants to talk with you. Each alert can divert attention to something way more exciting than an essay on the causes of the Civil War! Even beyond that, there are countless videos, pictures, TV shows, and interactive video games that can take a bite out of a teenager's homework or chore time. Hours of procrastination can go by and then the teenager is left with staying up late to finish work, doing a poor job just to finish, or not finishing at all. So how do parents help their children and teenagers learn to have good media habits?

> The process of developing a system for limiting technological distractions during homework time may be more "top-down" when kids are younger (parent decides) and more collaborative when kids are older. Establishing technology rules early on in your child's school career will be helpful for establishing good homework habits.

First, work together to establish ground rules about media during homework time. A firm "no media" rule will often be unrealistic. Some students really do need the Internet to complete school tasks. Some students will also claim that they use Facebook and instant messaging/texting to get information about school assignments from their friends, so they will need their phones or computers. However, a quick text to a friend about schoolwork can lead to a longer chat about a variety of other things. And there is only one click between a research article and a video of a dog riding a skateboard on YouTube. So unlimited access might not fit the bill either.

Talk with your teenager about what might be a fair way to allow access but prevent distraction. Some teenagers will agree to a cut-off point (no Internet or phone during homework time and cut off by 10 P.M. so that she can start to wind down to go to bed). Another might agree to do school-work in a common room so her parents can peer over her shoulder every so often to make sure she is using the computer for schoolwork. There is also the compromise of putting on parental controls that block social media outlets but not other sites.

Collaborate with your teenager about the rules and consequences for violating them. Starting with rigid restrictions may backfire, because adolescents are at the age where they want to be independent and make choices for themselves. Come to this choice together and you might just find more compliance.

Did you know that teenagers can restrict their own access to media sites? Your teen might be self-aware enough to know she needs to block out tempting websites. Some examples of websites that block access for certain time periods include *www.focalfilter.com* and software such as Anti-Social for Mac and Windows computers.

Another strategy that works for adolescents who do not have the self-control to stop themselves from engaging in social media or other diversions is to establish a "tech-free zone" in their homework area—no phones, no computers, no Internet. Then, if they need to use the Internet, they can borrow a family computer or a parent's laptop in another area. This creates a workspace where they are more likely to focus but doesn't inhibit them from using the computer when they need information.

Important Points to Consider

If your child is having difficulties starting tasks, before assuming that the problem is motivational consider that he may be having difficulties stopping a more desirable task or that the task may be too difficult for him.

○ Give your child a heads-up before he has to switch from one task to the next.

○ When your child is procrastinating, recognize that this can trigger a variety of negative feelings within you, such as frustration, anger, annoyance, or disappointment. Instead of responding immediately with sarcasm, nagging, or criticism, acknowledge these feelings, and consider that your child may be feeling similarly. Keep the lines of communication open on how to solve problems together.

○ Technology distractions are common culprits in procrastination. You can probably relate to the difficulty in putting aside technology to start on a less desirable task. Empathize with your child. Share times when you procrastinated and there were negative consequences, as well as a time when you put away technology to get things started and the positive consequences that resulted. Knowing that this can be a common challenge may reassure your child that there isn't something "wrong" with him.

 **CHAPTER 5**

Response Inhibition: Teaching Your Child to Control Impulses

Response inhibition is the ability to control impulses and keep oneself from doing the first thing that comes to mind. Children initially develop these skills by adults anticipating problems and, with words and actions, stopping them from acting. For example, if a young child is nearing a crosswalk, a parent might warn her that she needs to look out for cars and show her how to look both ways before crossing. As children develop, these controls become internal; children will be less reliant on adults to keep them safe and will think before acting. However, children and adolescents with response inhibition challenges may rely more on external controls and require more coaching to think through what they say and do. As a conscious parent, also be mindful of times when you act or say something before thinking. This is a common challenge, especially when a child's behavior is triggering your emotions. Practicing taking a step back and stopping to think about how you respond in these moments will show your child how to do the same.

The Importance of Controlling Impulses

Having response inhibition is necessary for safety issues with young children and adolescents alike. Children naturally love to run and climb around, and they need to be able to slow down and be safe when necessary. Adolescents need to be able to control impulses to do what might feel right in the moment (drinking alcohol, using drugs, having sex) and think of the long-term consequences.

In addition to physical safety, children and adolescents also need to control impulses in order to make and keep friends. Sometimes children with executive functioning deficits lack the "social filter" that keeps others from saying whatever comes to mind. Socially successful kids learn that their mouths do not need to say everything their brains think! Children with response-inhibition challenges might just say something insensitive to a peer, not out of malice but because of a lack of forethought as to how the comment may be received by the peer. Adolescents with impulsivity may suffer socially when they are using social media. For example, they may hastily post a comment to someone's Facebook page without thinking about the larger audience and how it will be interpreted. Instantly, one comment can create a firestorm of follow-up comments and unnecessary drama.

Teach by example. When your child observes you in a situation where you acted on impulse, such as yelling at someone who angered you or saying something that you didn't mean, acknowledge your mistake. Tell her that you didn't stop and think about what you were doing and what you would do next time ("Next time, I think I will take a deep breath when I am angry at someone and wait to talk to him when I am calmer.").

Children and adolescents with impulsivity can also be quick to respond to situations emotionally, and may even respond with aggressive behaviors. They may focus on only one aspect of a situation and lose sight of the context. For example, if a child feels like a peer is being unfair, or cheating in a game, he may flip the board game over and say he's done playing. A child with more impulse control might address the peer by asking if he remembered the rule, asking for clarification about what the peer is doing in the game, or asking a teacher or parent for help with the problem. Instead, the child with impulse-control issues focuses only on the unfairness and does not think about the other child's perspective or what steps could be taken to solve the problem.

Children with impulsivity can also be more physical than children without impulsivity. They may grab, touch, or get in someone's personal space on an impulse and not realize it is inappropriate or invasive until it is too late. One way to counteract this is to explicitly teach social rules, such as "Most people like to be one arm's length away from other people" or "Ask someone's permission instead of grabbing something."

Lastly, impulsivity can show up in academic situations. A child with response-inhibition challenges can frequently create problems in the classroom setting. She might blurt out answers, talk with her peers instead of working, use things without permission, grab and play with objects that she should not be playing with, or get out of her seat without permission. The teenager with impulse challenges may also talk out in class and engage in side conversations. She may also report a feeling of restlessness and feel that she needs to get up and move around. For both children and adolescents, impulsivity can impact actual work production and accuracy. Some students will fail to read directions carefully and do assignments incorrectly. They might think they know what to do before the direction is given and be off the mark. Others will read the directions but fail to pay close attention to detail and do the wrong thing, such as adding instead of subtracting, or reading the wrong page.

Children and adolescents with response-inhibition issues might also be impulsive when they read. They may make guesses about words after registering only the first few letters. They may read the words quickly but inaccurately. For example, they might see the sentence, "The king's crown was shiny" and read it as "The king's crowded was shiny" because they saw the "crow-" prefix and just guessed. This changes the meaning of the sentence and it no longer makes sense. Reading inaccurately and impulsively can therefore create reading comprehension issues.

Reading out loud can sometimes be helpful for children and adolescents with impulsivity issues. It can slow them down and also help them hear when they make mistakes.

Regardless of how impulsivity manifests for children and adolescents, there is evidence that teaching them how to delay gratification and manage their impulses will improve their quality of life. Several studies have been conducted that show the positive effects of being able to resist temptation.

Stanford Marshmallow Study

In the 1960s, researchers at Stanford University conducted a landmark study of young children and the benefits of being able to delay gratification. They put a child in a room with a one-way mirror so they could observe him, and gave him a marshmallow (or another treat). The child was told that he could have *two* marshmallows if he waited until the examiner came back in the room. The examiners then observed the child to see if he could control his impulse to eat the marshmallow. The children who were in this experiment were followed up on years later, and the children who were able to wait to get the second treat had better outcomes in life on a number of measures—SAT scores, level of education, and healthy weight. These studies suggest that response inhibition, or the ability to show self-control and delay gratification for a reward in the future, is an important executive functioning skill for success.

The "new marshmallow" in kids' lives today might be technology. Every time a phone or computer beeps to let you know that there is something interesting happening, it can be very challenging to ignore it. Even adults may find that it is hard to resist checking e-mail, voicemails, and texts during projects or tasks. But research shows that humans are not particularly adept at this type of multitasking. This constant switching of tasks interrupts deeper thinking skills and can end up setting the stage for poorer quality work, undetected errors, and lengthier time to complete tasks. Resisting the technology marshmallow may be one of the keys to successful completion of work.

You can build up your young child's inhibition skills in a fun way by playing games. Simon Says and Red Light, Green Light are two examples of games that teach a child to stop and think before acting.

Strategies for Kids Who Act First and Think Later

So what do you do if you have a child or teenager who struggles with response inhibition? How can these skills be developed and strengthened? There are a number of strategies for helping children with impulsivity.

ANTICIPATE

Children who act impulsively often have warning signs before they act. The signs may be fleeting, but they are there! Your job is to recognize these signs, which can include increasing frustration, agitation, or overexcitement. These feelings often lead to impulsive behavior. Each child will display the warning signs differently. For example, some children show their frustration in their facial expressions, while others may clench their fists, or sigh or make exasperated sounds. The key is to be aware of what your child's warning signs are. When you see a warning sign, you can redirect, prompt, remove the child from the situation, and/or encourage calming strategies. For example, if your child is playing a game and you can see her getting frustrated, you can step in and redirect her to take a deep breath or take a break from the game, or ask her to tell you in her own words what she is feeling. Or, if you see your son sighing and putting his head in his hands while doing homework, he might be on the cusp of rushing through his math worksheet just to be done with it. Your job is to take note of what happens just before the impulsive act and intervene. Eventually, you will want to teach your child to recognize her own signs so she can regulate her own behavior. Be explicit about why you are intervening, which will help her understand how to recognize her own triggers.

Sometimes children lack the vocabulary to express how they are feeling. If the child doesn't know how he is feeling, you might ask, "What are you thinking about right now?" to get some clues.

TEACH REPLACEMENT BEHAVIORS

Some children with response-inhibition challenges will do the impulsive act because they haven't practiced other behaviors they could do instead. For example, if a child is frequently grabbing your things without permission, you need to teach her what to do instead. So if you notice her taking something without asking, you can stop her and say, "Let's try this again. Can you ask me to use it?" Then, when she asks, you give the object to her to reinforce the asking behavior. If she isn't allowed the object, then you can redirect her to an object she can use ("My scissors are not for you to use, but I'd be happy to help you look for some child scissors so you can do your project.").

For blurting or interrupting, you will want to teach ways to politely enter a conversation. In the same way that teachers will only call on quiet children who have raised their hands, you too can ignore the behavior you don't want or redirect into the behavior you do want. For example, you can teach your child to say "Excuse me" when she wants to add something to a conversation by prompting her after she interrupts ("Can you say 'Excuse me' before you add your thought, please?"). You can also teach nonverbal cues, such as holding up the pointer finger when wanting to add something to the conversation. Model these verbal and nonverbal behaviors as well, and point them out ("See how I wanted to talk to my friend and she was already talking with someone? I went up to her, waited for her to stop talking, and said 'Excuse me.' That is how you get someone's attention."). Sometimes what seems obvious to an adult has to be explicitly taught to a child with impulsivity.

It is important to teach impulsive children and adolescents what to do, instead of what *not* to do. This can be done by changing your language slightly. Instead of saying, "Don't interrupt me," you can say, "Say 'Excuse me' when I am talking" or "Wait until I am finished talking, please." Then, the child will know what the desired behavior is.

CATCH THEM BEING GOOD

Children with impulsivity and response-inhibition difficulties are often stuck in a negative-feedback cycle. Most interactions they have with adults involve having their behavior corrected ("Don't talk out" or "Wait your turn."). This can put a strain on a parent-child relationship because there are fewer positive interactions. One way to counter this is to be on the lookout for desired behaviors. Whenever you see your child waiting patiently, be sure to comment on how much you appreciate her patience. Catch your child being good, label what she is doing as "good," and praise her. It is important to be specific ("I like how you didn't interrupt me when I made that phone call") and sincere. Children and adolescents can read through false praise easily. Really take the time to notice when your child is being in control, resisting temptation, or showing restraint.

When children act impulsively, they tend to need short redirection rather than long lectures. One or two sentences should do: "I need you to ask permission to use my things first. Can you ask first?" versus "Why are you always taking my things? I have told you over and over again! You need to stop doing that." Kids tend to tune you out during long lectures.

Strategies for Kids Who Make Careless Errors

In addition to behavioral impulsivity, there are children with response-inhibition problems who make careless errors in their schoolwork. These children will often skip directions, misread information, or begin tasks before they know exactly what to do, or they may jump into problems and then get lost in the steps.

LOOK FOR PATTERNS

The first step in helping children with impulsivity in their work is to identify the types of school tasks they have difficulty with. Does your child make more careless errors on math or on reading tasks? Does he frequently omit words when writing because he is so eager to get his ideas out? Are visually "busy" worksheets a problem for him? Do you see him not paying attention to the signs in math (addition versus subtraction)? Ask your child's teacher if the impulsivity leads to careless mistakes in all subjects or just in a few. That way, you can begin to identify patterns of difficulty that can be addressed.

TEACH SEQUENCES

Teaching procedures or routines for ensuring accuracy is one way to help children with impulsivity. Once you have identified the areas of need, you can teach a sequence that can be applied to similar assignments. For example, if your child has trouble with math word problems because he tends to skim the question, you could teach a sequence for solving word problems:

1. Read the entire problem out loud.

2. Draw a picture of the problem.

3. Circle the key words for clues about the math operation (*more than, less than, fewer, equal to, how many left*?).

4. Set up the problem.

5. Do the problem.

6. Check your work. Does your answer make sense?

As another example, for writing you could teach acronyms for proofreading so your child can remember what he needs to do after he has finished a piece of writing. A popular one is the "COPS" technique:

1. Capitalization: Check that the first word in each sentence and proper nouns are capitalized.

2. Overall: How is the overall appearance and readability (spacing, legibility, indentation of paragraphs, neatness, complete sentences)?

3. Punctuation: Is the punctuation correct? Do sentences have periods? Do questions have question marks?

4. Spelling: Is the spelling correct?

In general, sequences should be short and simple, between three and six steps. You can work with your child's teacher to reinforce sequences she may already be using in the classroom. Your child could have the steps on a Post-it or index card for reference at home and at school so he starts to build a routine for multistep problems.

ANTICIPATING

A good way to start teaching your child to anticipate the demands of a task before he jumps right in is to make sure that he fully understands the task demands. Often, children with impulsivity will not look carefully to see what they are expected to do. When your child is given a task such as a worksheet, before he starts have him read the directions out loud, look at the number and type of problems, and repeat back to you in his own words what he is expected to do. Then, after the task is done, check in to see if he has completed all the parts. This process helps children understand that they may have to slow down and think about what they are supposed to do before they start doing it, to avoid missing parts of the assignment.

HIGHLIGHT VISUAL DETAIL

Another strategy for students who are impulsive in their schoolwork is to draw attention to visual detail or key information. Highlighting is one way to go about this, but it must be taught explicitly (or you will have random things highlighted or too much highlighted). For example, you can have your child highlight the steps in a written assignment in different colors as you discuss each step. For math, you can have him go over each operation and color code it (for example, addition in pink, subtraction in yellow). Be consistent with the colors used and involve your child in the process of selecting which color matches which operation.

Children with difficulties with response inhibition are particularly prone to making mistakes on multiple-choice tests. This is because there are purposeful distractor items that seem correct but are not. Teach your child strategies such as reading *all* the items, even though she thinks she found the right one, and using the process of elimination to improve multiple-choice test-taking skills.

CHECK YOUR WORK

Many times, children with impulsivity and response-inhibition difficulties will not check their work. They are just happy it is done and they want to move on to the next thing. It is worth getting your child in the habit of checking his work. He can check that he did the assignment correctly, that he did all parts, and that his answers make sense. Teaching proofreading skills is another useful tool for checking work. You will want to develop a routine for checking work together with your child. Be careful not to be in the role of your child's "checker." You will want to engage your child in checking work for himself by guiding him through the routine, rather than doing it for him.

Important Points to Consider

Controlling impulses is key for social and academic success. Teaching your child "stop-and-think" skills will improve functioning at home, at school, and with friends.

O Explicitly teach your child what you want her to do ("Wait your turn") instead of just saying what you don't want her to do ("Don't interrupt me.").

O "Catch" your child when she is acting appropriately (being patient, asking permission to use something, waiting her turn) and praise her immediately.

O Look for patterns of mistakes (adding instead of subtracting, not using punctuation in writing) in your child's schoolwork and talk with her teachers about strategies to help with that type of mistake.

O Keep in mind that children, especially young children, learn by watching parents. Be aware of when you are about to act impulsively by identifying your triggers, such as frustration or anger, and choose a calming strategy. Describe to your child the strategy you used to stop and think before acting (deep breaths, expressing your feelings, taking a break). In this way, you are acting as a model for the behavior you want your child to do.

 **CHAPTER 6**

Focus: Everyday Mindfulness

In order to learn, you need to be able to focus. Research shows that the ability to focus is related to early learning skills, intelligence, language, and academic performance. Children and adolescents with executive functioning difficulties can struggle with several aspects of focus, including sustained focus and divided focus. Sustained focus is the ability to keep at a task long enough to complete it, whereas divided focus is the ability to manage several tasks at once. Research suggests that many of the tools conscious parents use—being present, aware, and reflective—are also tools that help children with focus issues. This "everyday mindfulness" can be infused into your family's lifestyle, even in our multitasking society where everyone seems to be on the go. Integrating mindfulness activities into your daily life will have the dual benefit of helping you be a calm and present parent and helping your child learn how to focus on one thing at a time.

What Do Focus Problems Look Like?

Common challenges with focus for children and adolescents include failing to pay attention to directions or needed information, missing important details in a conversation, having a hard time sticking with a task, and getting easily sidetracked while doing a task. You may find that your child takes in information much like you would a broken cell phone conversation—he gets part of the message but not all the details. You may also find that the littlest thing can derail your child from finishing his homework or a chore. In a world where technology rules an adolescent's social life (texting, instant messaging, video chatting, social media posting), you may also struggle to help your teenager finish his homework at a decent hour every night because he is constantly distracted. Learning tools for teaching your child sustained focus and managing divided focus will likely improve overall functioning.

A recent study in the *Computers in Human Behavior* journal indicated that teenagers and young adults average less than six minutes on a school task before switching to a technological distraction, such as checking social media or texting. Students who frequently accessed Facebook had lower GPAs than students who avoided it on purpose.

Sustained Focus

Sustained focus can also be thought of as attention span, or the amount of time needed to complete a task. Of course, attention span varies by age. Young children may have attention spans from a few minutes up to about twenty minutes, while teenagers may be able to focus for periods of up to forty-five minutes without a break. Children and adolescents with executive functioning challenges in focus may have much shorter attention spans and thus have to "reset" their attention more frequently.

SELF-MONITORING

One of the first strategies for improving sustained focus is to help the child or adolescent recognize when she is focused and when she is not. It might seem obvious to an adult when a child isn't focusing, but children are often unaware of what focus looks and feels like. Begin by having a discussion about what focus looks like, to give the child an image to hold on to. For example, during homework time, focus may look like the child seated in her chair, electronics off, work in front of her, eyes on the work, and body quiet.

The next step is to teach self-monitoring by giving your child opportunities to notice when she is focused and unfocused. You can practice this in several ways. You can set a timer at random intervals and when it goes off, your child can mark on a tally sheet whether she was focused. There is no reward or punishment involved; it is just to build awareness of what it feels and looks like to be focused. There are similar techniques that are more technologically advanced, including pagers that vibrate and phone applications that alert the child at random intervals. These tools can help your child reset her focus if she discovers her mind has wandered.

Make sure you are modeling how to avoid distractions. When you are having a conversation with your child, don't check your phone, glance at an e-mail that pops up, or do a chore at the same time. This will help you listen fully to your child and model active listening.

Older adolescents will likely not enjoy you hovering over them and monitoring whether they are focused! However, it is still important to teach teenagers how to self-monitor focus. The first step is to solicit buy-in to the idea of teaching them how to monitor their focus during homework and studying time. You might suggest that learning this skill will improve their grades, decrease homework time so there is more free time, or create less stress because you will not have to be monitoring them as much.

Offer to help in a coaching role instead of a monitoring role. Sometimes teenagers need an "accountability partner" whom they check in with periodically to keep themselves on-task. Have a discussion with your teenager about how you might best help her build awareness of when she is focused and when she is off-task.

THE POWER OF CHOICES

Adults and children alike know that it's easier to focus on something you enjoy or feel successful doing than on an undesirable task or something too challenging. This is why some children can play video games for hours on end or build elaborate Lego kingdoms all day long but can't seem to sit still and focus on their homework for long at all. Children and adolescents will also gravitate toward tasks they can do fluidly or with ease. It's more rewarding to do something well than to struggle to focus on something difficult. You can empathize with your child's struggles and offer support. She can choose to work with you, have an older sibling or peer help, research online supports, reach out to a friend doing the same task, or seek support from her teacher. By giving her options about how to seek help with a difficult task, you are empowering her to use similar problem-solving and coping techniques in the future.

Too much choice can be overwhelming for some children. They may look at all their choices and not know where to even begin! Start by providing two choices and then work your way up to more choices.

While children and adolescents may not always be able to choose to do a fun activity over homework, some choice in tasks is better than none at all. Choice leads to motivation and motivation leads to better attention. If you give your child a choice in which tasks she starts first, you may find some improved focus because she got to choose it. You can help your child with making choices by creating a homework or study plan and organizing the tasks in the preferred order. Then, after the homework or study session, you can check back in and reflect on her choices. Was it easier to start on something enjoyable? Better to get the hard assignments out of the way first? By asking these questions of your child, she may begin to ask them of herself as she becomes increasingly independent.

Divided Focus

Adults often call divided focus, or the ability to divide your attention and do several things at once, "multitasking." Multitasking (which is really rapid switching between tasks) takes executive functioning skills, and often children and adolescents are not equipped to be successful multi-taskers. Instead, they tend to be drawn away from the task they are doing and either do a poor job of finishing it, take a long time to get back to it, or forget to finish it at all. Studies have shown that using technology during studying for purposes unconnected to studying, such as checking e-mail or social media, is highly detrimental to learning new information as well as to applying learned information to new situations. A child's or adolescent's learning can be spotty or shallow as a result. Worse yet, students grossly underestimate the impact of media multitasking. This means they don't even realize how much learning energy is being stripped away, one text or one post at a time.

While popular sentiment may indicate that kids are good at multitasking because they practice it all the time, research is still showing that very few people (around 2 percent) can effectively multitask. Media multitasking in particular has been shown to have a negative effect on learning and grades.

The brains of children *without* executive functioning challenges struggle with divided attention, so the impact of multitasking on students *with* executive functioning challenges is likely much worse. Studies have shown that the brain simply cannot do two cognitively complex things at once very well. If the tasks are easy or "mindless" (such as listening to music while doing the dishes), that is a different story, because your brain doesn't have to compete for resources to pay attention to each task. However, when a child is doing two tasks that involve the same part of the brain, the competition for attention resources makes both tasks more difficult, makes both take longer to complete, and makes it harder for him to remember and deepen the learning. For example, when a student is trying to decide how to respond to a text and write a paper at the same time, his brain is using the same regions—the prefrontal cortex and language centers—to plan and organize what to say. Further, in this example, the student has to switch from informal text writing to formal essay writing, and this can put a strain on resources, causing mental fatigue and leading to more mistakes.

Instead of checking your phone or responding to texts, e-mails, or social media during an activity that requires focus, purposefully put your technology aside and show your child that you too can profit from being unplugged to get a task done!

Children who are prone to distraction must learn skills for focusing on one task at a time. So how can parents help? First, share and discuss the results of studies that show multitasking interferes with learning. Talk with your child about how children and teenagers who do not media multitask learn better and have better grades. Second, set up ground rules about studying time. Since these distractions are not going away, allow for media breaks after periods of sustained attention. Studies have shown that with practice, the length of time children can focus on schoolwork can increase. Start with fifteen-minute intervals, so that after every fifteen minutes of media-free studying, there is a short break (five minutes) in which your child can check his e-mail, texts, or social media. Gradually increase the time interval so that he has an opportunity to improve his attention.

TV or Not TV? There Is No Question!

In addition to social media and connecting with friends over technology, television and videos on the Internet are sources of distraction. Since most television shows do not have to be watched at a certain time thanks to DVRs, instant downloads, and streaming software, the temptation to watch a favorite show is fueled by the ease with which children and teenagers can get access.

In the same way that social medial drains attention resources, so do television and videos. Studies have shown that even background TV noise can be detrimental to focus and learning, even when you are not actively watching or paying attention to the TV. The noise and images from the television pull your attention away, even if you don't think they do. So turn off the TV when your child is in the same room doing homework, and remove or turn off the TV in children's bedrooms if they study in their rooms. Let your child know she can watch a show or look at a video when she needs a break or is finished with her work.

Music and Focus

Does music also have the same effect on the brain's ability to multitask? Many students report that they study better with music because it keeps things from being too boring. There are other students who like things library-quiet when studying. The research is somewhat mixed on music and concentration. What is clear is that the effects of music during studying and homework time depend on what is being studied and what kind of music is playing. In general, research shows that music has a negative effect on learning when you are studying something complex or something that requires memorization. Also, music with vocals is worse than instrumental music because it's a bit like someone talking to you while working—it uses up the language-processing parts of your brain, which you need for studying. There is some evidence, however, that music can improve one's mood, so during rote or mundane tasks that do not require high levels of concentration, it can make something boring more bearable. But the key is that the task must be very easy to do. Finally, listening to music *before* studying can improve mood and attention, so that might be a compromise when you are trying to get your teenager to turn off his music.

Mindfulness

Research has also shown that mindfulness, or the process of narrowing or widening one's focus intentionally, can improve attention and decrease stress. Some have likened mindfulness to yoga for the mind. Children with attention difficulties have tons of thoughts racing through their minds, making it difficult to focus on just one thing, such as doing a homework assignment, reading a chapter in a book, or studying for a test. You can teach your child to quiet her mind by repeating mantras such as "slow down," having her focus on her breathing, or creating a pleasant visual image in her mind.

Mindfulness practice has been shown to help children with focus and attention. Studies also show that it can alleviate symptoms of chronic pain, anxiety, and depression.

Consider adopting a daily mindfulness practice by trying it out for 10 minutes a day. This will put you in a better position to help your child find a mindfulness practice that fits him. Teaching mindfulness to your child is a bit like teaching your child to ride a bicycle—it's a lot easier to do if you have first-hand experience!

There are countless websites with ideas for mindfulness activities with children. The Association for Mindfulness in Education has a resources section that can direct you to activities to try with your child at *www.mindful education.org*. Experiment with different types of activities. Children may gravitate toward certain types of mindfulness. It's a matter of finding a few that your child likes. For young children, you may start with just a few minutes of breathing together. For elementary and secondary students, start with small intervals of five minutes and gradually increase the time up to about twenty minutes. This can be done just prior to studying and/ or during study breaks.

Adolescents may enjoy using technology to learn and practice mindfulness. For example, there are a number of commercially available apps that teach you how to meditate by focusing on deep breathing or guided imagery, as well as how to be present in daily activities, such as eating and walking. Headspace and Smiling Mind are two apps that may be a good starting place.

Important Points to Consider

Focus is essential for learning and successful task completion. Focus can be taught through modeling or by giving feedback about what focus looks like. Mindfulness practice (focusing on one thing, such as one's breathing, a visualization, or a sensory experience) can also help. Here are some other points you should keep in mind to help your child with focus:

○ Explicitly teach your child what focus looks like by telling him what behaviors you see when he is focused (eyes on work, feet and body still, etc.).

○ To teach self-regulation of focus, consider using a timer at random intervals; when the timer goes off, have your child report whether he was focused.

○ When your child has several tasks to complete, allow him some choice in what he has to focus on first.

○ Encourage your child to focus on one task at a time. Share the research with him that multitasking affects learning and grades in a negative way. Set up ground rules about media-free study time. Use media as a break, rather than have it available as an ongoing source of distraction.

○ Encourage and teach your child mindfulness—the practice of focusing on one thing for a period of time, whether it be on the breath, a mantra, or a visualization.

○ Be a good role model for focus. Put away your own distractions when you are listening to your child or engaging in a task. Practice daily mindfulness activities. If you are new to mindfulness, download an app that guides you through short activities you can practice. You may also want to learn and practice mindfulness activities with your child or teen.

 **CHAPTER 7**

Time Management: Strengthening Your Child's Internal Clock

Some children seem to have time blindness—they are almost oblivious to the passage of time and tend to think only in terms of "now" and "not now." When a child has trouble feeling the passage of time, it can create all kinds of problems. You may be familiar with the child who just can't seem to get out the door in the morning to be on time for school, or the teenager who suddenly needs a ride to an extra rehearsal but forgot to tell you she was supposed to be there fifteen minutes ago. Children and adolescents with time-management issues also struggle with projecting into the future and are therefore hurried or stressed, or give up on finishing tasks. The good news is that you can help your child develop "future vision," which will help her learn to feel the passage of time and anticipate the future to set goals. Learning to understand your child's challenges with time management serves a double benefit of strengthening her future vision as well as reducing family stress.

Development of Time Management Skills

One of the main skills for developing good time management is the ability to "see" yourself in the future. Young children have limited time horizons, and thus the skills for time management are developmentally bound. What this means is that how far in advance a child can anticipate an event in the future varies by age. In general, toddlers and preschoolers can think about events ranging from "right now" up to about twenty minutes from now. Elementary-age children's time projection ranges from a few hours up to about twelve hours, while adolescents can typically think ahead about two or three days. Knowing his developmental limits becomes very important when you are trying to teach your child to think into the future and visualize the possible outcomes of events in the present. Trying to get your eight-year-old to think about and plan for events two weeks from now may not be your best use of time!

There is a positive side of time blindness—the phrase "Time flies when you're having fun" is backed up by research. When you are internally motivated by and interested in a task, you can be unaware of time. Children and adolescents may describe this as being "in the zone." As long as being in the zone doesn't interfere with other tasks that need to be done, it can be a positive experience for your child.

Getting Out the Door on Time

A common problem for children and adolescents (and adults!) with time-management difficulties is being on time. This is because poor planning skills and difficulties with time estimation can make it difficult to leave the house with everything needed. You may find yourself running around in the morning trying to get your child organized for school; meanwhile your child is sitting in his room playing with his trains! Or you may observe that there are only five minutes left until you have to leave, and your teenager is just hopping into the shower. No matter how early you get your kids up, you may be perpetually late anyway. So how can you help your child learn how to get ready to leave without doing all the reminding and packing up of her things yourself?

VISUALIZATION

Children with executive functioning difficulties tend to not think of their behavior with the end result in mind. So when you say, "Get ready for school," they may not conjure up an image of what it looks like to be "ready." If they don't have a picture of what it looks like, then they won't be thinking of all the steps needed to get there. It's sort of like getting in your car to go somewhere and not thinking of where you want to go. It would be tough to plan out your trip without the destination in mind. Even though children have been "ready" many times before, they may not have been consciously aware of what it looks like. One strategy for helping children know what "ready" looks like is to ask them. You might be surprised at some of the things they omit—brushed hair, lunch bag in hand, backpack with homework in it, sports equipment—things that should automatically be a part of their getting-ready routine. Another strategy is on a day in which they are totally ready, take a photo. Then, you can post the photo near the door and reference it when you ask your child to "get ready" by showing her what it looks like. Or you can pull up the photo on your phone and show it to her. It may seem obvious to you what "ready" looks like, but for some children with executive functioning problems, it may need to be taught. If they knew what it looked like, then they would probably be getting ready without reminders of the steps every day.

THINK IN CATEGORIES, NOT CHECKLISTS

Children with executive functioning challenges often have problems in several different areas. For example, your child may have difficulties with both time management and memory. This means that your child may seem to be constantly running around trying to find her things in order to get out the door, and inevitably will forget something. Adults will often recommend use of a checklist, which works well for some children. The problem is, if your child also has memory challenges, a long checklist is too much isolated information to remember. Short checklists may be helpful, but if there are more than a few items on the checklist, it may be beneficial to group what your child needs to do or bring with her into categories. A few categories are easier to remember than ten or fifteen individual items. Just think if you went to a grocery store and things were not arranged by a common feature—dairy, meat, cleaning supplies, soups, cereals—you would take forever trying to find what you need. For the getting-ready process, some sample categories and the items associated with them might be:

○ **Personal Hygiene:** get dressed, clean face, brush hair, brush teeth, put on footwear

○ **Food:** lunch bag, drink/thermos, snacks

○ **School Supplies:** Backpack, homework folder, school books, pencil bag, permission slips, special projects

○ **Personal Items:** Keys, phone, wallet/purse, identification, money

○ **After-School Activities:** Uniform, equipment, special shoes

Using categories helps parents give cues to their children without having to go down a long list of everything they might need. Instead of "Do you have your keys? Your wallet? Money for lunch? Your ID?" you can just ask, "What personal items do you have?" and then remind your child if she missed one. This will also help your child to start mentally grouping the items she needs into the categories. You can also help her memorize the number of steps or items in a grouping (e.g., there are five things to remember in the "personal hygiene" category) so she will know if she missed any. You can also talk with your child about what items can be gathered up the night before and what items will need to be gathered right before leaving. That way, your child can do some of the getting-ready activities the night before, such as packing her school supplies or grouping her afterschool things by the door.

MEALTIME RULES

Children with time-management issues are notorious dawdlers. This can be a challenge when you are trying to get your child to eat a decent breakfast before leaving. She may be distracted during meal time by talking, playing with toys, texting/using her phone, finishing up homework at the last minute, or trying to decide what to eat. All of these activities can lead to lateness. If you have a breakfast routine at the table, set ground rules that there are no toys or electronics at the breakfast table. This will speed up the eating process and you won't have to keep reminding your child to eat.

If your child chronically does not eat breakfast, or becomes ill when you force breakfast, consult with your doctor. You might have to make special arrangements with your child's school that he can have a mid-morning snack so he does not go hungry.

Children's and adolescents' growing bodies and developing brains rely heavily on the regular intake of food. When kids skip breakfast, physical, cognitive, and behavioral problems can occur. Just think of how unfocused and cranky you can get when you haven't eaten! If your child claims she is not hungry, try to get *something* in her before she goes off to school. A balanced meal is best, a granola bar in the car on the way to school is better than nothing, and semi-starvation until lunchtime is not good at all!

If you are a fast-paced kind of person, you might respond with annoyance, frustration, or even anger when your child is not moving quickly enough. Instead of responding with exasperation, take a few deep breaths and make sure that there is a legitimate reason to rush your child. Stop and think of your own motives and consider your child's point of view. It may not matter to her that she finishes breakfast so you can get to Target before it's crowded. When you stop to think, it may not actually be a big deal, so try slowing down and enjoying the moment you are in with your child instead of worrying about moving her along.

Getting Homework Done Efficiently

Homework time tends to be a particularly difficult time for children with time-management difficulties. Difficulties can include distraction, procrastinating, underestimation of how long an assignment or project will take, avoidance behavior, and taking too long doing homework.

ELIMINATE DISTRACTIONS

The first step in building a more efficient homework routine is to eliminate distractions. This means providing a quiet and clean designated space for your child to work. Turn off background music and TV and ensure that electronics are not at the workspace. If you have more than one child, figure out if they can work next to each other or if they need to be in separate spaces. For teenagers, you may have to negotiate where they work. Some teenagers like to work on their beds, or spread out on their floor. This is fine as long as they don't end up falling asleep or doing something else in their rooms instead of homework.

With teenagers, it is important to approach changes in their homework routine with thoughtfulness and dialogue, rather than unilaterally imposing new rules. Teenagers want to be a part of the decision-making processes, and you will find that a new system developed together will be far more successful than an imposed one.

VISUALIZE THE END RESULT

Children with time-management issues often do not start with the end of homework time in mind. Rather, they focus on the possible negative emotion of the present time, such as worry, feeling overwhelmed wondering where to start, boredom, or frustration from giving up something more fun to start on homework. Help your child by asking, "What do you think it will feel like when you are done?" Walk him through what will happen when he is finished and help him imagine the positive emotion.

For example, you could say "Imagine you are finished with your homework. What are you doing? How are you feeling?" This can get him to think about the positive outcomes ("I get to watch my favorite show") or positive feelings about being done ("I will feel relaxed and proud of myself.").

MAKE PREDICTIONS

Part of the challenge in getting children to become more efficient with homework time is that they often do not have a good sense of how long tasks will take. Sometimes they underestimate and end up pushing off homework until the last minute and find themselves cramming to finish or staying up late. At other times, they overestimate how much time a task will take, and they avoid starting because it seems too daunting. You can help your child build a sense of time by writing down predictions for how long a task will take and then recording how long it actually took. This can be done for a week or so, just for information gathering. Then, you can go over the patterns with your child (for example, he takes longer on math than he expects; he is faster at writing assignments than he estimates). With this information, you can better plan for the length of time it will take to complete homework and make adjustments, such as working a day ahead on lengthier tasks, or zipping through quicker tasks to gain momentum. Whether your child prefers to start with the more daunting tasks to get them out of the way or with the easy tasks to feel accomplished is also something to explore.

ANALOG CLOCKS

There is something about an analog clock that helps kids feel the passage of time better than a digital clock. Perhaps it is the visual of the hand sweeping across the clock. One strategy for helping your child feel the "sweep of time" is to have an analog clock at his workspace. In order to help him understand how long he needs to work on a task, you can mark the clock with a Post-it or a magnet and tell him he needs to work until the big hand hits the Post-it or magnet. Then, when the time is up, you can check in on progress and reset the time. This can also be done to break up big tasks into manageable parts ("When the big hand hits the half-hour mark, you should be done with the outline of your paper") and schedule breaks ("When the big hand hits the forty-five-minute mark, we will take a short walk with the dog and then return to work."). Showing your child the sweep of time on the analog clock may help him get a feel for the passage of time and how efficient he is with his time.

It is important not to use this strategy as a punitive measure. If you find that your child is not done with the tasks at the stopping time, have a discussion about what got in the way, problem-solve together how to keep on track, and reset the time. This will teach your child to self-monitor and adjust effort.

USE OF TIMERS

Using a kitchen timer or timer on a smartphone is also a popular way to help kids stay on track during homework time. While it doesn't show the passage of time as well as an analog clock, it does work well for kids who like the idea of "beating the clock." You can have your child estimate how long it will take to finish a task and set the timer. When the timer goes off, you can check in on progress. Again, the timer is used for feedback about how effective your child was with his time, rather than a way to criticize when he wasn't effective. Use the timer as a way to have a discussion about what works and what doesn't for getting work done. You can also check your child's work for accuracy, to make sure that your child isn't just rushing through the task to get it done. Balancing speed and accuracy is another lesson that can be taught through this strategy.

While some children like the added pressure of a timer, some children become anxious about the time. They may lose focus on the task because they become preoccupied with the time. You know your child best. If after trying the timer you see him getting upset or anxious, the strategy may not be the best match for him.

TECHNOLOGICAL TOOLS

Using an app to keep track of how to use homework time is a good strategy to build time awareness. The app 30/30 (*http://3030.binary hammer.com*), for example, allows your child to break a big task into smaller parts, estimate how long each task will take, build in breaks, and will remind him about the sweep of time with a countdown clock. This tool can be particularly helpful for children and teenagers who tend to underestimate how long an assignment will take, because they get immediate feedback about how far they are and how much time they have left.

Teaching Activity Scheduling

For children who struggle with time management, it is crucial to explicitly teach them how to use a planner and a calendar. There are many different techniques and systems that can be used. Some children will like physical planners and calendars they can hold or see, and other, perhaps older children may enjoy online calendars or phone applications. The key is finding the one that makes sense to your child and one she will consistently use.

So many parents report that their child starts out using a planner and then abandons it after the novelty wears off. The key is to develop a consistent routine for checking the planner to make sure it is being used. You may have to collaborate with your child's teacher to ensure assignments are being written down.

THE PLANNER

The first step in helping your child manage her time is to teach her how to use an individual planner to keep track of homework, deadlines, tests, and other commitments. Whether the planner is a book or an online system will depend on your child's age and interest in technology. Regardless, it is important to have at least a week-at-a-glance format so that your child can anticipate tests and big due dates, as well as afternoon and evening commitments that may cut into homework time.

Do not assume that your child will intuitively know how to use her planner. Collaborate with your child's teacher to develop a system for making sure assignments are written down or imported, and check nightly to make sure the planner is in use. Have the child write "No homework" for individual classes in which she doesn't have homework that night, so you know that she didn't just forget to write it down. Also, teach your child to break up studying for a test into at least two nights before the test by writing "Study for test" as the homework. Finally, your child may enjoy using her planner more if she can color-code each class or subject. These colors can coordinate with folders and book covers of the same color to help her know which folders and books to bring home.

Many schools have homework websites that students can check nightly. This means that your child may not want to use a planner because it is redundant to write down assignments. In this case, help your child figure out which teachers consistently update and which do not, and help her develop some sort of system for putting long-term due dates on a planner or calendar, since they are not updated nightly on the homework website.

FAMILY CALENDAR

Keeping a family calendar and posting it where everyone can see it is a good way to teach time management and scheduling. Especially for busy families with multiple children and activities, having a visual aid is essential. It may help to color-code each family member's activity with a dedicated color, so at a glance, your child can see which obligations are hers. Be explicit and talk out loud when you are making scheduling decisions so your child can hear and internalize the thinking that goes into planning your family's time. Kids may also respond to stickers, Post-its, or magnets that represent certain activities. The beauty of movable parts on your calendar (versus writing and erasing) is that kids can visually see that plans change, but obligations do not typically go away; they simply move to other times. This can help children understand prioritizing.

Important Points to Consider

Take the time to understand that executive functioning challenges can have a real impact on how well your child is able to feel the passage of time. It probably isn't very pleasant to be rushed, late, and unprepared. Once you understand the nature of the challenge, seek to find strategies that will help him. Here are some other key facts to keep in mind:

- To facilitate good time management when getting ready to leave the house, help your child visualize what "ready" looks like. Encourage your child to conjure up his "ready" image before you ask him to get ready. For a younger child, you may want to take a photograph of what "ready" looks like and reference it the next time you ask her to get ready.

- Teach your child to think in categories of what he needs to be ready instead of in checklists. Categories may include personal hygiene, food, school supplies, personal items, and afterschool activities.

- Encourage your child to get items needed for the next day ready to go the night before.

- To keep your child from getting distracted during meals, enforce a ground rule that there are no toys or electronics at the table. You can also practice mindfulness activities such as drawing attention to the taste, smell, and texture of the food you are eating.

- Have your child make predictions about how long each homework task will take and check in afterward to see how long it actually took. Discuss the patterns you see with your child.

- Have your child use an analog clock rather than a digital clock at his homework area. You can have your child put a Post-it on the time he needs to work until so he can visualize and begin to have a better sense of passing time.

O Teach your child how to use a planner, whether it be a written one or an electronic one.

O Post a family calendar and refer to it to teach planning and time management skills.

O Be aware of your own motives and make sure you are not trying to make your child adapt to a different time schedule when there is no real need. In our fast-paced world, it is also appropriate to slow down and enjoy living in the moment with your child from time to time.

 **CHAPTER 8**

Working Memory: Hold That Thought

Working memory is the ability to hold information in one's mind long enough to process it, remember it, or act on it. It is also sometimes referred to as short-term memory. This is the memory you use when someone is giving you directions. He may say, "Turn left at the stop sign, go five blocks down, take a right on Elm Street, and then it's the fourth house on the left," and you have to hold all that information in your mind long enough to remember it, either by repeating it in your mind, writing it down, or visualizing the streets you will be taking. You do all of this while ignoring other thoughts that may come into your mind or outside noises that can pull away your focus. At times, parenting a child with working memory difficulties can be frustrating. You might feel as if you are constantly repeating yourself and directions are not followed completely. It may seem like your child is not listening to you at all. Understanding how working memory can impact your child and how to strengthen this skill and work around challenges is a first step toward reducing your and your child's frustrations.

The Importance of Working Memory

If you know what working memory entails, you can easily see how important this skill is for learning. At school, teachers give directions and students must follow those directions. In higher grades, teachers give lectures and students are expected to hold what the teacher is saying in their minds long enough to take notes.

Working memory is also instrumental in doing academic work. In reading, one must remember what is being read while thinking about how it relates to what was just read. Children and adolescents with working memory problems may forget the sentence they just read as soon as they move on to the next one. In math, one has to hold multiple steps in mind to complete problems. If a child has problems with working memory, she may get lost in the steps or forget the mental math she just did and write down the wrong number. And in writing, a student must be able to hold on to what she just wrote, what she plans to write, and how the ideas are related.

Did you know bilingual students tend to have better executive functioning and stronger working memories than monolingual students? According to research by Penn et. al (2010), even bilingual students with learning disabilities outperform monolingual students with learning disabilities. This is likely because they constantly have to switch languages and think flexibly about the words they will choose.

Studies have shown that working memory is an important executive function when it comes to overall intelligence. Students with strong working memories tend to learn more and be able to focus better in school. They are rated as less inattentive or hyperactive than their peers with working memory problems. It makes perfect sense. If you have difficulties holding information in your mind, you might tune out or get tired easily because it takes so much concentration to remember what is being said or shown to you. You may look around the room more, or get out of your seat, to see what other children are doing because you missed the direction.

The "RAM" in Your Brain

Psychologists have several different analogies to help explain the process of working memory. One useful analogy is to liken working memory to RAM (random access memory) in a computer. RAM is used to store random information on a temporary basis. Having more RAM is usually related to having a faster computer. In the same way, working memory stores information temporarily, and the stronger your working memory, the faster and more efficiently you can process information and store it in your "hard drive," or long-term memory. There are a few different types of working memory.

AUDITORY WORKING MEMORY

Auditory working memory is the process usually meant when psychologists describe working memory. This is the process of holding information in your mind that you hear. One way psychologists measure working memory is to give children a digit-span task. They tell the child to repeat back strings of numbers of increasing length (for example, 3-5-9-2). Then, they might ask him to do a more complicated working memory task, which is to remember the information in a different order, say in reverse order or from lowest to highest. The skills required to do this task include attention and concentration, as well as working memory abilities. The child must hold on to the information, filter out any distractions (in his mind or in the room), and process the information to say it back.

There are a variety of programs designed to improve auditory/verbal working memory through targeted practice, such as an online program with a coaching component called Cogmed. Studies show that younger children (under age ten) show significantly larger benefits from auditory working memory training than older children (eleven to eighteen years old).

These auditory working memory skills are essential in the classroom, because teachers will often give complex directions ("Get your math book and turn to page 217. But first put your name on the page. Then we will start with every other odd problem."). Or at home, you might give a multistep direction like "Go upstairs; get your socks, shoes, and laundry basket; put the basket in the laundry room; and put on your shoes and socks so we can go to the park." You might find your child barefoot, holding the laundry basket, and not remembering what to do next.

VISUAL-SPATIAL WORKING MEMORY

Visual-spatial working memory involves holding visual information in your mind for the short term. In our directions example, it would be as if someone showed you a map of where to go, and then took the map away and you had to hold that image in your mind. Psychologists sometimes refer to a "visuospatial sketchpad" in which the mind holds the image, and then like an Etch A Sketch, it disappears unless you do something to actively remember it, such as describe it in words or make efforts to visualize it for the long term.

Poor visual working memory has effects on academics as well. Students with poor visuospatial sketchpads may easily forget how letters and numbers are shaped or what correctly spelled words "look" like, or have trouble with remembering patterns, images, or graphics. Additionally, the visuospatial sketchpad is involved in navigation in space. Students with visualspatial working memory problems can have trouble with navigating around their classroom, school, or neighborhood because they lack strategies to pull up the image of where they are in their visuospatial sketchpads.

Remembering and Following Directions

One of the practical aspects of working memory is the ability to remember and follow directions. In general, the younger the child or the more impaired working memory is, the harder it is for her to remember lengthy directions. However, there are a number of strategies that parents can use to help their children with the working memory task of remembering and following directions.

REPETITION

No one likes to repeat himself over and over. And kids don't like to hear the same thing over and over and feel that they're being nagged! One strategy to avoid having to repeat directions and eventually ask the annoying question "Did you hear what I said?" is to instead have the child repeat back the direction you just gave. This way, you can figure out how much of the direction she really got. You might be surprised that even simple directions are misinterpreted or steps are forgotten. It is important to ask for repetition in a positive or neutral tone ("Can you tell me what I said so I can make sure you got all the information?") or else it can come off as nagging ("What did I say?!").

Model good listening for your child. When he is telling you something, stop what you are doing and give good eye contact. Then repeat back what you heard him say. This will show him what good listening looks like.

MANAGE DIRECTION LENGTH

For children and adolescents with working memory challenges, multi-step directions can be hard to follow. You may need to modify the number of steps in a direction by starting with one direction at a time. Then, when one-step directions are successful, you can build up to two- and three-step directions. In general, the younger the child or the more severe the working memory issues, the shorter the direction should be.

Working memory training can be fun! Instead of drilling your child to remember things, make it a game. For example, you can have your child help you remember three things at the store without writing them down, or see if she can help you remember the way to the store by being your "live GPS."

ACCOMMODATIONS

In addition to building your child's working memory by practicing repeating and following directions, you may need to accommodate her as well. Teach her to write down the steps in the direction. If she does not know how to write yet, you can write it down for her and have her read each direction to you. Or you can have her write a key word or draw a picture to remember each step. Experiment with where the child should write the direction. For a household chore or task where she will be moving around, she may write it on a Post-it or small piece of paper. If she is working on a homework task, she may write down the directions in her planner or on her computer's notes, reminders, or calendar function.

Remembering Appointments and Assignments

Just as adults need reminders and strategies for remembering important events and to-do items, so do children and adolescents. Children and adolescents with executive functioning challenges and working memory problems need them even more! Some kids also grossly overestimate what they think they can remember. These are the kids who say that they don't need to write things down, but then they end up not remembering the assignment. Or they may write down part of the assignment or the name of the assignment ("Women in History Project") but not the details, so when they get home, they don't know what part of the project to do.

When discussing ways to accommodate working memory challenges with your child, it may help to normalize the process for her. Saying something like "Everyone needs help remembering things from time to time. Even I have to write things down!" can make a child feel less self-conscious about learning new strategies.

The key message that you have to teach your child is that he cannot rely on his memory alone; he needs to write things down. You will need to explore with your child what system works best—a planner, an electronic calendar, smartphone applications with built-in reminders, a family calendar, or a desk calendar. The important thing is to involve your child in the selection of his system and check in daily to see if he is using it. You will also likely need to talk with your child's teachers and coaches about your system so they can support it as well.

Can You Strengthen Working Memory?

There is controversy in the field of psychology about whether your working memory is a fixed entity or if it can be improved with practice or other interventions. More and more, researchers are showing that you can train your brain to improve your working memory. However, other research shows that you only get stronger in the specific skill you are training in. This means that you can work on increasing the number of digits you can recall in a series, but it may not translate to better working memory overall.

New evidence is showing promising results in the area of improving working memory. Studies have shown that both exercise and mindfulness improve some executive functions, including working memory. Mindfulness in particular has been shown to reduce mind-wandering, which is helpful when trying to remember something!

On the other side, some studies show that working memory training improves other cognitive skills, such as reasoning, reading comprehension, and some aspects of intelligence. While work still needs to be done before there can be a definitive answer about whether working memory can be improved, evidence exists that teaching strategies to compensate for a weaker working memory is helpful for children.

PRIMING

One strategy for improving working memory is to prime your child for the information she is about to receive. This gives her a "folder" for the information in her mind. For example, you can say, "I am going to tell you three things you need to remember to bring with you when we leave. Are you ready for the *three* things? Your backpack, the permission slip, and your lunch." Or when reading a story to your child, prime him to think about a particular question or idea so when he is reading, he is ready to receive the information ("You are listening for clues in the story that tell us that the main character is planning something.").

Did you know that you can build your young child's memory skills by reminiscing about events with her? Studies have shown that preschoolers with mothers who talk with them about their day and help them remember details about what happened have stronger memories. This joint reminiscing has been shown to have positive effects on children's recall when they are older.

REHEARSAL

You probably use this strategy all the time without really being aware that it is a great memory aid. When someone gives you information to remember, you repeat it in your mind. Some children do not do this naturally, but you can teach them. Initially, they can repeat the information out loud, but eventually they can learn to say what they heard in their minds.

Working memory strategy training is helpful for all children but has been shown to be particularly helpful for students with learning disabilities. Students with teachers who frequently teach strategies, such as mnemonics, do better on academic tasks than students who are not explicitly taught strategies.

You can model this strategy for your child by saying information out loud to remember it, and then pointing out that you are doing this because it helps you remember.

CLUSTERING

Working memory is limited, even in people without executive functioning difficulties. Studies have shown that people can generally hold about seven isolated bits of information in their minds at once, such as the digits in a telephone number or a list of things to buy at the store. People can hold more if they practice or use strategies such as "chunking" information. For example, instead of remembering nine items in random order, you can better remember three dairy items, three frozen items, and three breakfast items. This principle of chunking is a good strategy to teach your child. The "power of three" is also a way to teach chunking. If you can consistently group whatever it is your child has to learn into threes, then she will likely start to think in groups of three and become more aware when she is missing something.

There are a number of commercial working memory training programs, many of which are very expensive and in early stages of being researched for effectiveness. You might be better off starting with less expensive ways to improve memory, such as classic games—Simon, Memory, Concentration, Bop It!—until research is clearer about which programs are effective.

MNEMONICS AND ASSOCIATIONS

Another way to remember information is to create a mnemonic, which is a clever way to remember information, such as an acronym, poem, or song about what is being learned. For example, "PEMDAS" is an acronym for teaching the order of operations in a math problem (**P**arentheses, **E**xponents, **M**ultiplication, **D**ivision, **A**ddition, **S**ubtraction). Or, to remember the order of colors in the rainbow, one can take the first letter of the color and make it into a sentence, such as "**R**yan **O**ffers **Y**ou **G**reat

Bargains In Venice." Research shows that children (and adults) learn information better when it is funny, in song, or meaningful/relevant. This is why it is important to help your child come up with her own mnemonics. The more involved your child is in creating the memory aid, the better the chances she will remember it.

VISUALIZING

The brain takes in information through the five senses—vision, hearing, smelling, tasting, and touching. The brain is better able to recall what is learned if it gets information from more than one sense. This is sometimes referred to as multisensory learning. When a child or adolescent is learning material for a test, for example, he would profit from both hearing and seeing the information, and perhaps even participating in an activity or experiment that demonstrates the information. When studying at home, you can teach your child how to pair learning modalities to strengthen learning. For example, you can pair visual and auditory information by looking at videos of what your child is learning. Since there are countless videos on the web, it may be too much to simply give this suggestion and let your child search. He could get distracted and next thing you know, he's watching a music video or videos of kittens on YouTube! Check out *www.pbslearningmedia.org* for a clearinghouse of educational videos sorted by grade and subject to start.

BUILD RECALL, NOT RECOGNITION

So often, children and adolescents think they are "studying" when really they are just looking at study materials. There is a big difference between being familiar with the material you are studying and being able to recall the material on a test. Take studying vocabulary or spelling words, for example. Your child may recognize the word *perfunctory* but not be able to define it or spell it. If your child is studying something that requires recall alone (versus deeper analysis), then there are a few strategies that may help. For example, if he is studying vocabulary, you can encourage him to make flashcards with the word on the front and the definition on the back and quiz him. Some children, and particularly adolescents, prefer using an online program called Quizlet (*www.quizlet.com*). They can create their own online flashcards or look up other students' flashcards that have already been made on the same topic and quiz themselves online. Practicing with flashcards, whether they are handmade or online, can help build recall instead of just recognition.

If your child is expected to recall information *and* apply it in a new way, then the study techniques for memory will need to be deeper than flashcards alone. Types of tests that require more-sophisticated memory and learning are short-answer and essay tests, math tests, and multiple-choice tests that require analysis of several closely related but slightly different concepts. These types of tests tend to occur in the higher grades, but elements can crop up in the early grades as well.

One strategy that can help your child is to create or use a study guide to narrow the focus on what to study. Children and adolescents with executive functioning difficulties often do not know what to study or how to study. A study guide can help them. If the teacher does not provide one, you can help your child look through his textbook and pull out main themes by looking at chapter headings and subheadings and key concepts that may be in bold in the textbook. Ask to see your child's notes and go over them with him to get clues about what might be important concepts to know. You can also teach your child to advocate for himself—for instance, he can ask the teacher if she would meet with him before the test to go over his homemade study guide to see if important information has been overlooked, and to get tips on how to study for the test.

Memory is one part of the studying equation. Teaching memory strategies is a good first place to start. However, you will also need to make sure your child is understanding the material and not simply memorizing the words or procedures. If you get the sense that there is poor comprehension, you might need to seek extra tutoring in the subject area.

ELABORATIONS

One final strategy for remembering information for the long term is elaboration. Elaboration is a strategy that helps the child link new information to something he already knows. These associations help the child remember information. This is why summarizing, or discussing what one has read in relation to personal experience, is such a popular intervention for improving reading comprehension and memory. It helps the child elaborate on the information.

One can also elaborate visually on information, such as by using imagery. You can tell your child to picture what is being learned or read as if it were a movie. Or, if he is learning a new word, he might picture the word in his mind. For example, when learning the Spanish word for chair, *silla* (pronounced *see-ya*), he might picture a person on a chair waving goodbye and saying "See ya!" Once again, the more involved your child is in developing these personal elaborations, the better the chances are that he will remember them. You may need to provide some examples and training to help him understand the concept of elaboration first, and then coach him on creating his own associations.

Important Points to Consider

Working memory challenges can be frustrating for children and parents, because learning, listening to directions, and following through with instructions may not seem to "stick" no matter how many times information is repeated. Teach your child strategies like the following to boost and work around memory issues and you will begin to reduce frustration.

O When your child fails to follow through with a direction, you may become angry or annoyed. Before acting on your feelings or criticizing your child for not listening, make sure she in fact heard all of the direction. In a neutral tone, ask her if she can repeat back what the direction was to make sure she understood all the parts. If she did understand and remember the parts, then ask if she needs help with any of the parts.

O Shorten complex directions by providing the steps one at a time.

O Teach your child to write down the steps in lengthy directions, either on paper or on an electronic device.

○ Prime your child's memory by telling her what to listen for before you give a direction or information.

○ Teach memory strategies such as chunking information (thinking of information in categories rather than individually), mnemonics (memory aides), and associations (clever ways to remember information).

○ Help your child remember better by encouraging multisensory studying techniques, such as pairing visual and auditory information or showing her how to link new information to something she already knows.

○ For rote memorization, teach your child how to use flashcards or online games such as Quizlet that will build recall, not just recognition.

○ Encourage your child to make a study guide by reviewing her notes, textbooks, and supplementary materials and, with your help, pulling out important concepts.

○ Encourage exercise and mindfulness practices, both of which improve memory.

 **CHAPTER 9**

Flexibility: Rolling with Changes

Being adaptable to one's environment is an essential life skill. Life is not always predictable, and children and adolescents need strategies to cope with unexpected problems or events. Being able to think flexibly is the key to solving problems that may arise, whether it be a new math problem, a change in routine, or a social challenge on the playground. Having a child who is inflexible can be trying, even for the most patient of parents. Understanding the executive functioning weakness behind the inflexibility may help you "listen with different ears" when your child is being rigid and testing your patience. When you frame the difficulty as a skill that needs to be taught, versus framing his behavior as him being oppositional, you may be better equipped to provide the emotional support your child really needs in the moment.

What Does Flexibility Entail?

There is an invisible process that occurs when your environment changes—your mindset also changes. The process of shifting your mental state and behaviors based on changes in the environment is called cognitive flexibility. It is also sometimes called set shifting. Psychologists test this skill by giving children and adolescents tasks that require looking at a problem in many different ways and not getting stuck on one way. For example, a child may be given cards with pictures that can be grouped by many common features—such as color, size, type of animal, or shape—and be asked to sort them in as many ways as he can. Children with executive functioning challenges in cognitive flexibility might sort them in only a few ways or repeatedly sort them in the same way. This process can play out in real life too—these children can spend forever on one problem, trying the same inefficient strategy over and over, or think there is only one way to solve the problem.

Being flexible is an adaptive skill, in both academic and social realms. Flexible kids are more liked by peers as well as adults. Things change all the time and there are many unexpected surprises (good and bad) that can change the course of the day. Problems can result when kids struggle with these normal changes. When the movie in their head about how things should go takes an unexpected turn, they can often have strong emotional reactions and dig in their heels, holding on to their idea of how things should be. Children and adolescents with flexibility problems are sometimes described as "rigid" or "inflexible." They might also be described as "my way or the highway" kinds of thinkers. But instead of viewing them as oppositional and willful, it might be more useful to think of them as having delays in their ability to think flexibly. These skills can be taught.

Parents who are looking for strategies for teaching flexibility to children who present as oppositional may find the work of psychologist Ross Greene to be helpful. His work centers on the Collaborative Problem Solving (CPS) approach, and his website (*www.livesinthebalance.org*) offers great techniques and resources.

Another aspect of cognitive flexibility is the concept of social flexibility. Part of social flexibility is the notion that we think about the ideas, feelings, and actions of others. For people without social flexibility problems, this seems perfectly obvious. But for many children with executive functioning problems, particularly those identified as having autism spectrum disorders, this is a thought process that is not automatic or natural. Children with social flexibility problems may only consider their own vantage point, which creates a problem when things don't go their way or when someone asks them to do something that wasn't their own idea.

The ability to take another person's perspective and to understand that others have different thoughts, feelings, and intentions than your own is called "theory of mind." Children with difficulties with theory of mind tend to have flexibility issues because they tend to consider only their own viewpoint.

For example, if a child is working on a drawing and you say it is time to go to school, he is not thinking that you want him to be at school on time, or that the teacher is expecting him, or that if you don't get him to school on time you will be late for work. He is only thinking about wanting to do his drawing and may become upset when he has to stop. Or, if a child is on the playground and wants to play soccer but everyone else wants to play basketball, she might get upset because she is focused on what *she* wants to play. When we think about what others are thinking, it allows for more flexibility.

Social thinking is a term coined and popularized by Michelle Garcia Winner. Her website, *www.socialthinking.com*, offers curricula, books, workshops, and other resources on how to develop social thinking and cognitive flexibility.

Learning How to Reset

In the both the academic and social worlds, children and adolescents with cognitive flexibility challenges often get stuck on one way to do a task. You may find that when your child is stuck on a homework problem, you get resistance when you offer to help because it's not the way the teacher taught the problem. Your child may even have a strong emotional reaction to being asked to do things differently, even when it is in the spirit of helping her get unstuck. In the social world, you may find yourself offering advice about how to solve a social problem that is not well-received. For example, you may ask your child, "Why don't you play the game your friend wants to play this time, and then next time you can play a game you want to play?" and be met with a meltdown.

STRATEGIES FOR GETTING UN-STUCK

Children and adolescents with cognitive flexibility challenges will often get stuck on one way of solving a problem, whether it is a problem on their homework assignment or a problem on the playground. In the academic realm, parents will often struggle with how to help their child when she is stuck on an assignment and is resistant to help. For example, a child may be working on a math word problem that is in a slightly different format than what was taught in class. She may try to complete the problem using the steps given in class and find that they do not work in this particular problem. Yet, instead of trying it a new way, she continues to try the same steps. She may even become upset when you try to teach her a new way of setting up the problem and say, "That's not how the teacher taught it!" Or, in the social realm, during a play date your child may make up his own rules to a board game and refuse to play by any other rules. He may also get upset if he's building something and the other child tries to join in and "messes everything up."

One strategy is to provide an opportunity for your child to "reboot." You may even use this analogy with your child, depending on her age and ability to understand metaphors. Sometimes computers get overloaded and they keep spinning but they don't get anywhere. In these cases, it's best to just reboot. The same can be true for when your child is "spinning" on the same inefficient strategy or is stuck on her own idea about how things should go. Encourage your child to take a five- to ten-minute break, doing something different, and return to the task or the situation later.

It is important to also teach your child calming strategies; otherwise, breaks will do no good. The first step in teaching calming strategies is modeling. When you become overwhelmed, frustrated, annoyed, or feel any other range of emotions when doing your work or a household task, stop and label the emotion for your child's benefit. You can say something like "Wow. I am getting really frustrated with installing this application on my computer, and I can feel myself getting angry and confused. I am going to take a five-minute break and come back to it." By showing your child that it is normal to get frustrated, but that you can take a break and return fresh to tackle the problem, you are teaching her a coping strategy.

You can also label your child's feelings for her, particularly if she doesn't have a large bank of feeling words or doesn't use them when upset. By labeling, you are grounding your child's experience. It is important to also label with empathy. So instead of "You're mad. Would you just take a break!" you can say, "I get the sense you are feeling mad, which is okay. I understand. I sometimes get mad when things aren't working the way I want them to. It might help to take a little break and come back to this." This way, you are normalizing the feeling and providing a strategy to try.

Recognize that the feelings of anxiety and disappointment that accompany the challenges of doing something a different way are real, even if you don't see why the event should be that upsetting. Think about a time when you were upset that something didn't go as planned and imagine that feeling magnified—that may be how your child is feeling.

If taking a break is not sufficient, you may also want to encourage self-talk or "thought-stopping." Sometimes children and adolescents with difficulties with flexibility will get stuck on a thought that keeps them spinning. These thoughts will typically have a "should" or "shouldn't" in them—like "I should have all the puzzle pieces" or "She shouldn't mess with my blocks" or "I should do this math problem the way my teacher taught me." You may need to help your child come up with a new thought to say to herself to get unstuck. For example, change the "should" to a "sometimes" proposition. So, alternatives might be "Sometimes others will share my puzzle/blocks and it's okay" or "Sometimes there is more than one way to do a math problem."

Teaching new ways to think about events and feelings is a core feature of cognitive behavioral therapy (CBT). This type of therapy teaches children and adolescents that their thoughts control their feelings, and that their bodies give them clues about their thoughts and feelings. Thought-stopping is one technique, among others, that can be helpful for teaching new ways to cope with issues.

There are also a number of ways to teach your child about flexibility in social situations. You can start with integrating the idea of flexibility into play. For example, when reading books, if a character is flexible or changes his mind and there is a positive outcome, then you can point it out and talk about it. You can take some Play-Doh that is hard and dried out and Play-Doh that is soft and malleable and ask which is more fun to play with. When playing with building blocks, you can do an "experiment" to see what it would feel like for you to rearrange them for a while in a new way. If your child gets upset, you can use it as an opportunity to encourage coping strategies such as labeling, self-talk, and thought-stopping.

Changing Plans Midstream

For children and adolescents with cognitive flexibility challenges, changes in routine can be upsetting. They may want to take the same route to school every day. They have a strong preference for "sameness"—the same

> Recognize that some children, particularly those on the autism spectrum, will profit from visual support for changes. You might tell *and* show your child how things will be different, by showing a picture or video clip of a child going through the same change, reading a story about a child coping with changes, or moving pictures of activities in his visual schedule.

jacket, the same lunchbox, the same order of doing tasks, the same food. They may get upset when there is a change in family plans, or a change in the school schedule.

One way to help your child cope better with changes and become more adaptable is to provide anticipatory guidance for changes. If you know that it will be a shortened school day and your child will be getting out of school early, or that there will be a substitute teaching his class, let him know in advance. If you planned on going to the store but you realized you needed to pick up your younger child from daycare first, prepare your older child for the change in plan. Talk about the change and you may be able to prevent him from getting upset that you are driving the wrong way. If there is a big change coming up, such as beginning a camp, starting or ending school, or family members visiting, put the change on the calendar where your child can see it and start talking about how things will be different a few days or weeks in advance.

> Sometimes it may seem easier to just give in and do things the way your child wants to do them. However, in the long run, it is better to teach the skill of flexibility. Pick an inflexible behavior that you want to change and start with small, manageable steps. You can also allow some opportunity for him to do things the way he wants in a creative way—a special art project, a building project—so that he can have a sense of control in one area, but in an area where it is okay to be somewhat rigid.

There may be instances when you cannot anticipate a change. In these circumstances, it is best to help your child access his coping skills. Acknowledge the feeling (disappointment, anger, confusion, worry) and encourage positive self-talk ("I can cope with changes; I have done it before" or "Things change, but I will be okay") and visualization of a positive thing that may come out of the change. You can build these coping skills into your daily routines in small ways, so if a big change happens, your child will be better equipped to handle it. You can take slightly different routes to school; add small variability to clothing, food, or toy preferences; and help your child adjust to the small change.

Repairing

Sometimes, despite best efforts, a child with cognitive inflexibility will have a meltdown because something didn't go as planned. In these situations, you will want to start with calming your child down. The time for discussing what she should do differently is not when she is in the heat of the moment. Think about a time when you were extremely upset. You are not always able to process things logically in this heightened state. The best time to process the incident is later, when your child is calm again. It may even be best to let the incident go until a quiet time later that evening. It is important to talk about it in a constructive way. Start by empathizing with your child ("I know you were very upset this afternoon during your homework time."). Ask her how the event made her feel and provide feedback to show you understand ("I hear that you were mad that you couldn't do your report on elephants. That must have been disappointing."). You do not necessarily have to agree with the fact that your child got mad about something that didn't seem like a big deal to you. The important thing is that it felt like a big deal to your child and you want to find out her experience. Then you can talk about problem-solving and coping skills ("The problem is, elephants were already taken by a classmate and the rule was that each student has to do a different animal. I understand you didn't like the rule, but there is a way to solve this problem and we can figure it out together."). Finally, if there was inappropriate behavior to address, you can do so in a way that teaches a coping skill ("It is okay that you were angry about this, but it was not okay to rip up the assignment and throw it at me. Can we think of another way you can show you are mad that isn't hurtful?"). Each time you walk your child through this sequence, you are building coping skills.

When children are upset, parents often respond with anger, and then try to use logic and reason. However, when a child is angry or flooded with a big feeling, the logical side of her brain is often shut down. Make sure you are calm before you intervene. Acknowledge your own feelings and then try to see things from your child's point of view. Before using reason with your child, start with reflective listening and acknowledge the feeling ("I understand that this doesn't seem fair. I will be here for you and we will figure out how to make you feel better together."). This process is sometimes called "time in," because you are helping your child process the emotions together, instead of leaving her to manage them on her own in "time out."

Important Points to Consider

Change can be difficult for all children but especially for those with executive functioning issues. You will need to be there to support your child and be open to his questions and concerns no matter what they might be. Remember that children with flexibility problems view things in a more concrete way than others of the same age and so they have trouble adjusting to change. Try to be patient and understanding of your child's unique needs. Here are some things to consider:

O Introduce the concept of "rebooting" with your child when he gets "stuck" on an ineffective strategy for solving a problem or is fixated on an idea about how things should be done. Encourage him to take a break and reboot.

○ Teach calming strategies your child can use during reboot breaks, such as deep breathing, taking a short walk, doing a mindfulness activity, listening to a favorite song, etc.

○ Teach your child feeling vocabulary, and help him label his feelings when he is stuck.

○ Teach self-talk and thought-stopping techniques for when your child gets stuck. For example, change "should" statements to "sometimes" statements.

○ Read stories about children who are flexible thinkers and discuss them with your child.

○ For a child who gets upset when there is a change, provide anticipatory guidance or a heads-up if there is a known change in schedule so he can mentally prepare for it.

○ Make small, manageable changes and teach your child how to cope with them. This will prepare him for bigger changes.

○ If your child has a meltdown about a change or wasn't able to do things his way, use the process of "time in," which is modeling calmness and kindness, responding with empathy, and staying with your child until he is calm. Then, after he is not in a heightened emotional state, you can process with him what happened and how to deal with it in the future. Responding in anger, giving a "time out," or relying too heavily on logic in the emotional moment may be counterproductive.

CHAPTER 10

Self-Regulation: Thinking about Thinking

One of the goals of both parenting and teaching is to help children develop into independent thinkers and learners. Teachers hope that children will begin to take what they know and extend it, or think about a topic in a new way. Parents strive for children to take responsibility for their learning and complete tasks on their own. This process of self-regulation, being able to monitor one's thoughts, feelings, and behaviors to achieve a learning goal, is one that can be challenging for children and adolescents with executive functioning difficulties.

What Is Self-Regulation?

What does it mean to be a self-regulated learner? Self-regulated thinking is not the process of teaching yourself. Parents and teachers often serve as mentors for developing self-regulation in children by encouraging self-reflection, self-evaluation, self-monitoring, goal-setting, planning, and help-seeking. Self-regulation is the process that learners go through to plan, perform, and reflect on their learning in order to achieve their learning goals. Students who are able to self-regulate their learning do better in school, have greater confidence, and develop more independence in their learning as they get older.

> Of all the strategies for self-regulated learning, there are two that have been shown to have the greatest benefit on learning outcomes: taking practice tests and studying a little bit at a time over a long period instead of cramming.

Children and adolescents with executive functioning difficulties often struggle with self-regulation. They might jump into tasks without thinking ahead, and become prone to making mistakes. They might not know where to start on an assignment or project, get stuck, or give up after a setback. They also might seem to have trouble learning from their mistakes and continue using ineffective or inefficient strategies.

An important component of self-regulation is metacognition, which is "thinking about thinking" or "knowing about knowing." Parents have an important role as metacognitive mentors. Parents can help teach their kids to be more strategic, self-reliant, and flexible in completing academic tasks. Some of these skills parents do instinctively—offering ideas about how to get ready for an assignment; giving information about the structure of the task, the level of difficulty, or how to tackle the assignment; and identifying possible obstacles and strategies for getting around them. When children and adolescents get this type of instruction, they tend to have better self-regulation and be more successful in completing the assignment well. What parents might not know how to do is to explicitly teach specific metacognitive strategies for reading, writing, and math.

Self-Regulation in Reading

There are three main components to reading: word reading (decoding individual words), fluency (quickness, fluidity, and accuracy of reading), and comprehension. At each level of reading, there are strategies to help children and adolescents think about their reading process. These metacognitive reading strategies serve to help children and adolescents self-monitor when they are reading and use strategies to make sure they understand what they read.

VISUALIZING

When children and adolescents struggle with reading individual words, or with reading fast enough to remember the beginning of a sentence or paragraph by the time they reach the end of it, they need strategies to catch themselves when they are making mistakes. One strategy is to teach your child to visualize what she is reading while she is reading. She might picture what she read as if it were a movie, after each sentence, paragraph, or page. If she can't picture it in her mind, then chances are she made too many mistakes or didn't read fluently enough and needs to go back and reread.

Younger children may enjoy drawing what they read. For example, if your child is reading a story, you can have her draw the beginning, middle, and end. You can fold a piece of paper into thirds and she can make a picture of what she remembered from the beginning, middle, and end of the story. Or you could have your child draw what she thinks the character looks like based on what she read. For both of these strategies, if your child struggles to draw something, it may be because she didn't read for enough detail the first time around. You can help her go back and reread sections of the book to increase her understanding and ability to visualize what she read.

MAKING CONNECTIONS

Students with metacognitive difficulties in reading will often read accurately but not really be active in thinking about what they are reading; that is, they will "read" the page but not really be thinking about what it means. To help them become more active while reading, you can teach them to make personal connections to the text. Young children will start out making text-to-self connections, and you can prompt them by asking questions about how the material might relate to them ("What would you do if you were in this character's position?" "Does this passage remind you of things you have seen or heard before?" "What is your favorite part of the story and why?"). Older children can be prompted to make text-to-text connections (connecting what they have read before to what they are reading now) or text-to-world connections (connecting what they are reading with events in the real world). These connections help children and adolescents understand and remember what they are reading.

You can either have a discussion about what they are reading or have them annotate the text with their connections. Some parents and teachers have students write their connections in the margin of their own personal copies of books or textbooks. Some e-readers have built-in annotation devices as well. Or you can give the student a "metacognitive log" or "connection log" in which she can write down her connections. There are a number of different ways to encourage her to make connections to what she is reading, including T-charts (one side of the chart is for facts that she read, and the other side is for what she thinks about the facts or connections she made) and sentence-starters ("I think . . ." or "This reminds me of . . ." or "This makes me think about . . ."). Teachers and parents can provide the sentence starters in advance of reading, so she can write down her connections as she reads. Younger kids who are not yet fluent in writing can also engage in making connections through drawing pictures of what they read or telling you what they read while you write down their ideas for them.

QUESTIONING

Good readers are constantly thinking about what they are reading. They might ask themselves questions before, during, or after the reading process. Before they read, they might ask themselves, "What do I want to learn?" or "What is the purpose of me reading this?" This helps guide their reading and helps them focus. For example, if they are reading for fun, they might not have to memorize many details. But if they are reading to study for a test, they might be asking themselves, "Is this important enough to be on the test?" They might also review something they already read to find a specific piece of information or to understand something deeper. You can teach your child to think about the purpose of what she is reading, and this will help her change her strategy (skimming versus deep reading, scanning for particular information, or reading all the information).

Readers with good metacognitive skills may also ask questions in their minds during or after reading ("What does the author mean by that?" "What does this have to do with what I learned in class?" "What does this part mean?"). To facilitate this process, parents can encourage their children to question what they read. You can have your child ask you a question about the page or chapter she read and then the two of you can answer the question together. Or you can have your child put a Post-it on the part of the text that she has a question about and either research it together or encourage her to ask her teacher the question in class. This will help your child remain active in reading the text and also encourage self-help skills.

Scientists are researching whether reading online and reading physical books are different experiences in the brain. There is some evidence that "deep reading" of books (versus "informational reading" done online) is more satisfying and engaging because the brain actually immerses itself in the story and processes it as if were really happening.

MAKING PREDICTIONS

Particularly with younger children, you can help your child engage in thinking about reading by asking questions as you read together. One fun way to do this is to have your child make predictions about what will happen next. This will get her to start sifting through what she has read already for clues about what is to come. You can make guesses together, and then see if you were correct and talk about what clues led you to be correct or incorrect. These skills will help teach your child the important skill of inference—the "reading between the lines" skill. This skill becomes increasingly important as reading becomes more nuanced and full of metaphors, idioms, and figurative language.

Self-Regulation in Writing

Writing is a complex process that requires executive functioning skills—one must plan what to write; organize writing ideas; execute the writing in a timely manner; think about the audience and purpose of the writing; and use correct grammar, punctuation, and spelling as well as proofread, edit, and revise. Students who do not think about their writing process tend to produce disjointed and unorganized writing fraught with errors. The good news is that you can help support the writing process by teaching and reinforcing good metacognitive writing strategies.

PLANNING WHAT TO WRITE

The prewriting phase is very important for developing good metacognitive writing strategies. Planning out what to write is often a challenge for students with executive functioning deficits. You can help in this process in a number of ways. First, you can simply discuss the writing prompt with your child to get him to start thinking about the topic. Ask him what he knows about the topic and what his ideas are, and talk out a few ideas together. Second, you can help to organize these ideas in written form. Kids who tend to think linearly or in a sequence may prefer an outline form. Other kids profit from organizing their ideas in a more visual or artistic format. Graphic organizers are visual representations of what will be written and are a great way to organize ideas before writing. Examples of graphic organizers are flow charts, T-charts, diagrams, mind maps, Venn diagrams, and the like. There are a multitude of examples online that you can print and try with your child. You may also ask your child's teacher for examples of graphic organizers that are used in class.

You may also research graphic-organizer software, which allows your child to drag and drop visual images representing writing ideas; the program then helps them organize the ideas in an outline format. An example of such a program can be found at www.inspiration.com. Just click the Visual Learning tab and then select Graphic Organizers.

MENTAL CONTRASTING

Children and adolescents with executive functioning challenges in writing may often experience writer's block, in which they do not know where to start or they get stuck in the middle of their writing and are not sure how to finish. One of the ways to prevent these challenges is to encourage a prewriting activity called mental contrasting. In this strategy, the student is asked to write about the process he will undergo when writing an essay or a report. He writes two positive things that will come out of finishing the writing task and two potential obstacles. Then, he writes a series of if-then plans ("If (obstacle), then I will (plan to overcome obstacle).". Lastly, he plans out when and where he will do the task. This simple prewriting activity has been shown to increase task persistence and completion of tasks. This can also be extended to other types of projects besides writing projects, because it teaches children to visualize the future and plan for challenges.

MODEL WRITING SAMPLES

Sometimes the blank page can be daunting for children and adolescents with executive functioning challenges. They may not know where to start, or they may not be able to visualize what the writing should look like when it is completed. They may just write what comes to mind, and as a result their writing can be disorganized. One strategy that can help children and adolescents understand the writing process better is to show samples of the writing they are expected to do.

Be careful that your child doesn't just copy the model writing. To prevent this, look at the model writing and highlight core features—topic sentence, three main points, a paragraph for each point, elaborations on each point, a conclusion—and then have your child talk about how her writing will have each feature.

So, for example, if your child has to write a book report, ask the teacher for a good example of what one looks like so your child can see the parts he needs to do. Or, for an older child, you might ask the teacher if there is an example of a persuasive essay or a compare/contrast essay so your child can see the features of a good essay in the style he will have to produce. Looking at models of writing will help your child better understand the parts of the written work so he will know where to start.

RUBRICS

In addition to looking at good examples of different types of writing, you might also ask your child's teacher if there is a grading rubric that can help guide the writing process. A rubric is a set of expectations for the writing piece that is laid out in advance of the assignment, so your child will know what his writing is being graded on. So, for example, your child's writing may be graded on organization, spelling/grammar, use of rich vocabulary, author's tone and voice, use of transition words, etc. If you know in advance what is expected of the writing piece, then you can use the rubric to guide your child, as well as proofread the final product with the rubric in mind.

Some students are more expressive when talking about their ideas than when writing their ideas. Dictation software, which translates voice to text, may be a good alternative for these students. Dragon and Windows Speech Recognition are two examples of such software.

ORGANIZATIONAL STRATEGIES

Children and adolescents with executive functioning difficulties may have trouble connecting their ideas to a central thesis or in relation to other sentences they have written. One way to help children organize their ideas is to make the writing process more kinesthetic by having them write down ideas on cards and physically move the idea cards into categories in a logical order. Start by helping your child generate a thesis. A good thesis is one that has a position and outlines a few things that the writer will be discussing. For example, if your child is writing on whether schools should have uniforms, he might take a stance on the issue in his thesis and cite three reasons why. Have your child put the three main ideas on index cards. Then you can have him write his ideas and facts on other index cards, as many as he can think of ("Kids should have individual freedom. I wouldn't want to wear a uniform." "What if kids can't afford to buy the uniform?" "Statistics on how many schools require uniforms."). Then, have him put the ideas that relate to the main idea under the index card with the main idea written on it. This sorting activity can help a child work through and understand how supporting ideas, facts, and elaborations are connected to main ideas and the thesis.

Self-Regulation in Math

There are several building-block skills for math, and these skills are essential for understanding high-level math concepts. First, children must acquire number sense, which is the understanding of quantity, more/less, and ordering of numbers. Next, children must learn basic computation skills, such as basic addition, subtraction, multiplication, and division facts. Then these facts become automatic, and kids can use them quickly. This math fluency is essential for high-level math because knowing math facts frees up mental energy to focus on the problem instead of on the operations in the problem. Lastly, children learn math procedures, such as how to set up a word problem, how to solve for X, finding the area of a triangle, computing a proof in geometry, etc. Embedded in this entire process is the building of math reasoning, in which each skill in math builds on the next and a deeper conceptual understanding of math is the result.

Children and adolescents with executive functioning challenges can struggle with math for a variety of reasons. Some students will have working memory difficulties that keep them from developing quick and automatic math facts, or from holding one part of the problem in mind while doing the next. These students may make simple math errors, or work an entire word problem correctly but then forget the main question and give the wrong answer. Other students with cognitive flexibility challenges may get stuck on a problem if it is slightly different than the way the concept was taught. And yet other students with organizational challenges may get lost in multistep problems or fail to write down the steps needed to show their work and come to the correct solution. And finally, students with self-regulation challenges will likely make errors and not even detect them. There are a number of strategies to support self-regulation in math.

Some studies show that the strongest predictor of growth in math is surprisingly not intelligence but a combination of perceived control (beliefs such as "I can get better at math"), intrinsic motivation, and deep learning strategies (versus superficial ones like trying to memorize math problems instead of understanding the math concept).

PRACTICING BASIC MATH FACTS

Knowing basic addition, subtraction, multiplication, and division facts and having them readily available is called math fluency. This is why elementary school teachers are constantly drilling math facts—if you know them, it frees up your mind to focus on the math concept you are learning. If you are spending all your mental energy performing the operations, you might lose sight of the overall process or make simple math errors that can ruin the whole process. Children with executive functioning challenges, particularly those who struggle with working memory, may struggle with math fluency.

Parents can help with math facts in a fun way. In addition to the classic flashcard games, where parents show a math fact and their child tells them the answer, there are a number of games that can be played to improve fluency. Online games show a lot of promise, mostly because they are more engaging than basic "drilling" exercises. You can also teach and reinforce math skills through music modalities. For example, there are a number of "skip counting" songs to teach multiplication. Skip counting is the process of knowing multiples of numbers (for example, 3-6-9-12-15) so that you can quickly figure out the multiplication operation. Music is processed in many different parts of the brain, and as anyone who has had a jingle or song stuck in her head knows, it can be powerful for memory!

Operation Math by Spinlight Studio is a math fact app for the iPad, other Mac devices, and the Nook e-reader that is full of different "missions" for your "secret agent" child to accomplish. The app has settings for easy, medium, and hard problems, so your child can experience success.

BREAKING DOWN THE PROBLEM

Parents can assist with math homework in a variety of ways. Studies have shown that the manner of instruction at home can help children and adolescents self-regulate not only at home but also at school. The type of instruction that is most helpful for children and adolescents is to break a big problem into a series of smaller steps. This reduces the "cognitive load," or the amount of mental energy one has to expend in order to solve a problem. You can also help reduce cognitive load by setting an appropriate pace. Some kids will want to rush through the task and will make errors, so you can help slow your child down by emphasizing each step. When you take things one small, manageable step at a time, give feedback, and discuss progress on each step, you are teaching your child self-regulation.

Parents of adolescents may find that they are not able to do the math that their teen brings home, because they never learned the concept or it was too long ago to remember. Khan Academy is a free online tutorial program that you can direct your teen to in order to get a step-by-step breakdown of math problems at *www.khanacademy.org*.

PROBLEM-SOLVING SEQUENCES

Parents can also help children understand how to solve math problems by teaching problem-solving sequences. Children with executive functioning problems will need explicit instruction in this area, as they may not "talk" themselves through math problems. They might just see a problem and start plugging in numbers without giving much thought to the process. Teaching a sequence will help them better understand that there are consistent steps to math problems that one must go through to get the correct answer.

One such problem-solving sequence is this mantra: Understand, plan, do, and check. This sequence is general enough to apply to many different types of math problems:

- ☐ **Understand:** Read the direction or problem. Rephrase the problem or state what type of problem it is ("This is a subtraction word problem" or "This is a problem that is asking me to do the order of operations.").
- ☐ **Plan:** Ask yourself, "What do I need to do to solve this problem?" or "What are the steps in this problem?" Then answer those questions ("I need to set up the math sentence" or "I need to use the PEMDAS strategy.").
- ☐ **Do:** Complete the steps in the problem and show work along the way. Talk out loud or to yourself about the steps as you do them ("I am going to draw a picture of this word problem first to better understand what it is asking me to do" or "I am going to start with the operations in the parentheses.").
- ☐ **Check:** When you are finished, ask yourself, "Does my answer make sense?" Double-check your math operations and steps to make sure you didn't make careless errors, such as dropping a negative sign, or adding instead of subtracting.

There may be other problem-solving sequences that your child or adolescent's teacher uses in class. If there is a different sequence that your child is practicing, you can ask the teacher so that you can reinforce the concept at home.

Developing Self-Regulation

One of the best interventions for boosting academics is boosting self-regulation. It may surprise you that young children can learn how to self-regulate their behavior through play. Specifically, teaching kids to engage in extended pretend play has been found to increase executive functioning skills, vocabulary, academic test scores, and attention span, and decrease disruptive behaviors. So put away those flashcards and get out your firefighter hats and princess wands and get busy!

The Tools of the Mind program is a promising intervention in the schools that teaches kids executive functioning skills through play. Find out more at *www.toolsofthemind.org*.

The importance of play has long been discussed and researched by developmental psychologists. In addition to providing children with a nonverbal outlet for expressing feeling, it allows for creativity, imagination, cooperation with others, and opportunities for problem-solving, as well as a way to practice skills they will use when they are older. If you watch young kids play together, you will see them imitating their parents and each other (playing house is a good example). They take on roles and trade roles with each other, and they work out what is fair and who gets to play with what first. Make-believe play also allows kids to think of different ideas, story themes, and symbols—a process called divergent thinking. Before your very eyes you can see a child's rich imagination flourish during make-believe and fantasy play. Play is the universal language of children—every kid in every culture does it without being taught how.

So how can play lead to self-regulation? One of the interesting cognitive features of play is that it requires abstract thinking. If your child is playing house, for example, she is taking objects and pretending they are something else (that toy block is now a spatula) or using objects that are not real and imagining they are (those plastic eggs are real eggs and I am going to "eat" them). Kids also use abstract thinking when they take on roles during play. Your child might imagine how a mommy would react to a mess in the kitchen, and she might need to remember that her younger brother is the daddy and talk to him differently when in character.

Imaginative play can be helpful for older children as well! You can encourage storytelling, drama, creative writing, or fantasy card or role-playing games to support your older child or adolescent's creative side.

Kids also engage in self-reflection during play. They might ask themselves, "What would Mommy make for lunch in this play kitchen?" or "If I wear this crown, does that mean I am in a princess role now?" or "If you are pretending to be Spider-Man, then maybe I should pick a superhero to be too." They have to think about their roles in relationship to others.

In this day and age, there are times when kids' play gets cut short. Schools have shorter recesses, kindergarten is more academic than it used to be, and kids have less downtime because they are being shuttled off to organized sports or activities. While sports and activities are great, they are organized by adults, so kids don't get much practice in organizing themselves, a skill that can build executive functioning. Some kids are also constantly being entertained by TV, videos, and video games. These activities may not be "bad" in and of themselves, but they are more passive activities for the developing mind than creating an imaginary world under a fort of sheets. As a parent, you may also be tempted to keep your child busy and switch activities when she gets bored or restless. You may be inadvertently denying your child the opportunity to get creative.

According to the Kaiser Family Foundation, the average child ages eight through eighteen spends more than seven and a half hours per day behind a screen for entertainment—either a TV, computer, iPad, video game, or phone. This time does not include the time spent using a computer for homework or research!

So how do you help foster pretend play with your young child? Research has shown that parents who talk to their children about social situations and read or tell them stories tend to have kids who engage in more pretend play. Having a few dress-up items and toys that lend themselves to taking on a role may also help children pretend play. Finally, encouraging your child to play and make up stories, guiding your child to play, and joining in on her pretend play can foster the type of creative play that is helpful for developing self-regulation skills. For example, the Tools of the Mind program has teachers develop a "play plan" with kids (such as playing firehouse) and then have the children write, draw, or dictate this plan to them. This gets them thinking about the tools they will need for the play (firefighter's hat, hose, truck) and what roles they will each have. The process of thinking ahead and sticking to their plans are some of the precursors for self-regulation.

Important Points to Consider

Teaching self-regulation in school subjects can be intimidating. Don't feel that you need to learn how to be a learning specialist for your child. Your job is to support where you can and know your limits where you cannot. Enlist the help of specialists if intervening in homework time is causing strain on your relationship with your child. Sometimes it is best to be a parent, and not try to play the role of teacher if it's not working out for you and your child. Here are some other helpful pointers:

○ Teach your child to visualize what he is reading while he is reading. He might picture it as a movie, or draw what he read, for example. Teach your child how to make personal connections to what he has read.

○ For younger children, encourage them to make predictions about what will happen next in the book. Teach them how to look for clues about what is to come and make guesses.

○ Teach good prewriting strategies by discussing the topic first. Ask your child what he already knows about the topic, questions he may have, and his ideas for writing. From there, you can teach him how to make an outline, or encourage him to create a graphic organizer.

O Ask your child's teacher for examples of model writing in the genre in which your child has to write. Go over the core features of the genre and help your child understand the parts he will have to do.

O Ask your child's teacher if there are rubrics for written work. This way you and your child will know what aspects of writing are being focused on and what he will eventually be graded on. This gives structure and a guideline for the writing piece.

O Practice basic math facts in a fun way, such as with online games, apps, and by making math musical.

O Help your child break down a math problem into manageable steps and emphasize and discuss each step as you go through it.

O Teach problem-solving sequences that help kids talk through the steps needed to do a problem. One such sequence is the "Understand, plan, do, and check" sequence.

O Understand the connection between play and self-regulation. Encourage your young child to engage in make-believe play and imaginative play. You may even make a play plan with your child and talk about the materials needed for the play and the roles that you will take on.

 **CHAPTER 11**

Emotional Self-Control: Learning Coping Skills

The ability to control one's emotions is key in positive learning outcomes and daily functioning. Studies have shown that children and adolescents with more emotional self-control do better in school. This makes intuitive sense, because if a child is in control of her feelings, she is better equipped to learn because she is not distracted emotionally. She is better able to reach out for help when upset and can self-soothe and get back to work. At home, she can accept rules and consequences and handle negative feelings, such as disappointment, anger, or sadness. Part of learning how to parent consciously is to be more aware of your own feelings and how you react to them. By modeling calmness and kindness under stressful circumstances, you can teach by example.

Why Emotional Self-Control Is Important

Children who have challenges with emotional self-control are often easily overwhelmed and overreactive, and can feel out of control. When children and adolescents experience emotions that they feel they cannot handle, they will often resort to acting out. You might see angry outbursts, excessive crying, or tantrums. You may also see withdrawal behavior or shutting down—when your child retreats or refuses to interact or talk with you.

Learning to monitor his emotions leads to empowerment for your child. When a child has strategies for feeling in control, he is better able to handle the next negative emotion he has. That is, he will have a "tool kit" of coping skills that he can use in a variety of situations. Just think about a time when you were frustrated, overwhelmed, or angry, and imagine that you didn't have a strategy to deal with these emotions. It is a very uncomfortable place to be. Giving children and adolescents tools for self-monitoring emotions is one of the first steps to help them develop emotional self-control. Being able to recognize the strengths and types of emotion they are experiencing helps children and adolescents decide which "tool" they need to use to cope, and can reduce feelings that the emotion cannot be managed.

Instead of focusing on how to control your child's feelings, try to understand the root of the feeling. Is she disappointed, frustrated, angry, self-critical, or annoyed? The external behaviors you see are often a mirror of your child's inner landscape. Listen to her feelings, validate them, and offer support ("I understand you feel frustrated. Can you tell me what you need in this moment?").

The Tale of Phineas Gage

Children with executive functioning challenges often experience difficulties with managing negative emotions. Why? The answer comes from a man named Phineas Gage. In 1848, a young railroad worker named Phineas Gage suffered a horrible accident in which an iron bar went through his brain's frontal lobe. Remarkably, he survived, but he experienced emotional and behavioral volatility after the accident. His moods changed quickly, he could not stick to plans, he used foul language, and he was rude toward others. While scientists are still debating the accounts of Phineas's behavioral change, what is clear is that emotional self-control is related to frontal-lobe functioning, particularly in the orbitofrontal cortex. This means that if you are a child with executive functioning challenges, which are centralized in the frontal lobe, it may not be only academic self-control that is affected—emotional self-control may be lagging as well.

Labeling Feelings

One of the first steps in teaching emotional self-regulation is to teach feeling vocabulary. Most children will have a basic feeling vocabulary—mad, sad, scared, and happy—but as adults, we know that there are many more-nuanced emotions. The differences between feeling annoyed and furious, disappointed and devastated, or excited and terrified warrant different reactions and require different coping skills. To build this feeling vocabulary, you can start with modeling. When you are experiencing an emotional reaction, label it for your child and talk out loud about how you will cope with it ("I am feeling disappointed that our picnic has to be cancelled because of the rain because I was really looking forward to it. I'll try to think of a fun indoor activity" or "I am so frustrated that we are going to be late. I am going to take a deep breath and tell myself that it is going to be okay. I will call Grandma and let her know we'll be late.").

Upset is a word that can have many underlying meanings. One can be upset because of anger, sadness, or fear. Help your child clarify what he is feeling by asking, "Can you tell me what upset means?" or "Which type of upset are you feeling— mad-upset? Sad-upset? Scared-upset?"

You can also teach feeling vocabulary through books. There are countless books that teach children and adolescents about feelings. Even if the book is not geared in particular to teach feelings, you can talk about characters in books and their emotions as you read together. You can ask your child to think of a time when she felt the same way as the character in the story, or how she would have handled her feelings if she were in the same situation.

Finally, when you see your child experiencing a negative emotion, you can help build awareness of feelings by labeling it for her. You will want to approach this with a curious stance, rather than telling your child how you think she feels. This is called the notice-and-explore technique. You might say, "I noticed that after I told you we couldn't go to the zoo today you broke your crayons. I am wondering if you might be a bit disappointed or angry. Can you tell me more about what you are thinking about?" or "I see you are crying and you seem upset. When I cry, it is because I am sad. What is going on for you?" By noticing the behavior and then exploring the attached emotion, you are helping your child make the connection between events and feelings. Labeling the emotion often grounds a child in her experience, and helps make it something she can deal with. You might even remind your child of a time when she coped with the negative feeling before ("Remember when we didn't get to go the zoo before and you were disappointed, but then we ended up having a good time at the park?" or "Remember the last time you were sad and you sat and talked with me and it made you feel better?").

Providing Behavioral Choices

There may be times when your child's emotions get the better of him. Say, for example, you are in the grocery store and you tell your child he cannot have a candy bar. He might grab the candy bar anyway and throw himself on the ground, kicking and screaming. What do you do? First, you validate the emotion (even if you think it is a huge overreaction—it feels real to your child) by labeling it ("I see that you are upset that I told you that you can't have the candy bar. I know this must feel disappointing to you since you really want it."). Then provide a clear direction about what he should do instead of the negative behavior ("I need you to put the candy bar back and stand up."). You might also say something like, "It is okay to be disappointed or angry, but it is not okay to throw a tantrum" and repeat the direction. If possible, try to model calmness in yourself. Use a firm and confident voice, relaying that you believe that your child will follow the direction. Your child may not comply the first time, but continue to give the direction until he does.

There may be occasions when he still does not comply and you might need to intervene physically (if you can). Before you do so, offer a fixed choice, such as, "You can put the candy away and stand up on your own or I will help you do it." Then, if he doesn't comply, you will have given him a choice that you can talk about later, when he is calm. If the child is too big to physically move, you might need to wait out the tantrum. Now, of course there are times when you are exasperated or you cannot ignore the behavior because doing so would create a problem for those around the child. In these cases, you might need to negotiate. This is a last resort! As much as possible, it is important to not give in, or you are teaching the child that a tantrum gets him what he wants.

When your child is acting out, it is hard not to take it personally or think she is just acting out to manipulate you. But no child wants to act badly and disappoint her parent. She is acting out because she doesn't have any other tools to do things differently. Think of each tantrum as a teachable moment.

On the other side of the emotional continuum from acting out is when your child turns inward. The child who is crying hysterically or retreating to his room when he experiences something seemingly minor also needs help making good behavioral choices. Sometimes it is okay to let him take time to calm down alone, and sometimes it is better to stay with your child to help him calm down. You know your child best, and you can gauge what to do. You can even ask your child, "Do you need some time to calm down alone or would you like me to stay with you?" This choice empowers the child to express what he needs in that moment.

Tracking Emotions to Build Awareness

Children with emotional self-regulation difficulties profit from frequent check-ins about how they are feeling. Tracking positive, negative, and neutral feelings will enhance feeling vocabulary as well as build awareness of the connection between events, thoughts, and feelings. Once children are able to express how they feel, they are better able to handle their feelings. Think about a time when you tried to change a behavior, such as increasing working out or quitting a bad habit. One of the first things you might have done was track how much of the activity you were presently doing. This builds awareness and motivation for change.

A simple way to track feelings with your child is to come up with a chart that represents a range of emotions. You can start with tracking one emotion and add more as your child gets used to the chart. For example, you could start with anger, and draw a stoplight with red, yellow, or green feelings—red represents an angry outburst or strong anger feelings such as being furious or enraged, yellow represents mild angry feelings (annoyed or frustrated) that may lead to stronger ones, and green represents no angry feelings. You can ask your child to point to the color she is feeling at various points during the day, when you see her experiencing mild feelings, or you can reference the chart as a way to "debrief" after a behavioral incident, showing how she moved from green to yellow to red. The frequency with which you check in with your child will be dependent on how often you are seeing the negative emotion. Some children do well with a morning, afternoon, and evening check-in, whereas others may need more or less frequent check-ins.

A number of commercial programs are available for purchase that teach feeling vocabulary and self-regulating emotions by categorizing the way kids feel. One such program is called the Zones of Regulation at *www.zonesofregulation.com*. There is a curriculum as well as an application for mobile devices.

Another system for check-ins is "feeling thermometers." You can draw a thermometer for each of the major emotions—anger, sadness, happiness, and fear—and mark levels on each, bottom to top, from 1 to 10. One represents a low amount of the feeling and 10 represents the strongest feeling. Have your child show where on the thermometer she is feeling for each emotion and identify the events or thoughts that went along with that emotion. For example, your child may show that she was a 5 on the anger-feeling thermometer when her teacher kept her in for recess and she thought it was unfair. This can start a conversation about the feeling and begin problem-solving discussions about fairness and how to behave so she earns recess.

You can also track positive emotions, such as happiness, being excited, cheerful, or relaxed. This will help your child think positively and instill gratitude for the good things that happen during her day.

Dealing with Meltdowns

Parents of children and adolescents with severe emotional-regulation challenges will likely be familiar with meltdowns. There are times a child's emotions are so strong that he has an extreme emotional outburst. This may take the form of a tantrum, extreme crying, yelling, throwing, or even aggressive behaviors including hitting, kicking, or biting. When your child is in this state, it can be very difficult to calm him down.

Part of the work in dealing with meltdowns occurs before the meltdown even happens. Start with clear expectations for your child's behavior. While specific family rules can vary greatly in their detail, there are three core rules that might be a good starting place. Many of the family-specific rules can be put in these three categories:

1. Be safe.

2. Be responsible.

3. Be respectful.

When your child breaks one of these rules, it is worth reminding him of the three family rules, and you can tell him which one was broken. For example, if he starts throwing his things in anger, you can remind him that he needs to be safe. If he curses at you, you can point out that this behavior does not follow the family rule of being respectful. On the flip side, and perhaps more importantly, when you see your child engaging in a positive behavior, you will want to point it out! For example, if he puts away his things unprompted, you can tell him he is being responsible. Or, if he disagrees with you but does so in a polite way, you can point out that you appreciate how he was respectful even though he was angry at you. These reminders will help your child become more aware of his feelings and behavior, and this is the first step in self-regulation.

A great source for ideas about how to help your child learn a new behavior instead of doing a problematic behavior is the Positive Behavior Interventions and Supports website at *www. pbisworld.com.*

The next step is to try to ward off the meltdown in the first place. Most parents know when a meltdown is coming on, because there are frequently predictor behaviors before the incident. You might see your child tense up or notice a facial expression that indicates he is getting upset, or you might recognize a triggering event that will likely lead to an emotional reaction. If you see any of these predictor behaviors, try the notice-and-explore technique of making an observation about what is happening and asking about what the child needs. It is important to remain calm and neutral in your approach, if possible. This shows your child how to be calm even in the face of negative emotions. It is also a way to show your child empathy and understanding.

Children on the autism spectrum often have difficulties expressing themselves in words, and they tend to think in pictures. In order to process emotional reactions, or to prevent emotional outbursts, you may want to show your child social stories about how other kids react to events. A good place to start is the Stories2Learn app by MDR available at the iTunes Store.

If a meltdown cannot be avoided, then the next step is de-escalation. De-escalation is the process of bringing the child back to a calm state. The process starts with acknowledging where the child is coming from, either through the notice-and-explore technique or by simply labeling the behavior and emotion you are seeing. You can validate the feeling ("I understand why you may be mad") even if you think the child is overreacting, and then provide a few behavioral choices.

If your child's meltdowns create a situation where she is a danger to herself or others, the first priority is safety. If the child is at risk of hurting herself or others, then you might need to call 9-1-1 or a child crisis hotline right away. After the intervention, you can have a discussion with your child about the reason you called—to keep her and others safe. That way, she doesn't think she was in trouble for having strong feelings and losing control.

After the meltdown, you might want to take some time before processing the event with your child, as talking about it might ramp him up again. When he is truly calm, you can begin to ask questions about what led up to the meltdown, and how it may be prevented in the future. If a family rule was violated in the process, you might also provide a natural consequence for the behavior (if he tore up his sister's coloring book, he needs to replace it; if he said mean things to his sister, he needs to apologize). Keep in mind that your child does not *want* to feel emotionally out of control; it is a scary place for him. Punishing him beyond the natural consequence of the event may make things worse and send an inadvertent message that it is not okay to have strong feelings. The message should be that it is okay to have strong feelings, but it is not okay to break the family rules of being safe, respectful, and responsible.

Important Points to Consider

In order for your child to gain emotional self-control it is important for you to teach her more than just basic feeling vocabulary (*sad*, *mad*, *happy*, or *scared*). Teach the range of emotions and nuanced emotion words as well, like *annoyed* versus *furious*. This way your child will be better able to communicate with you the exact emotions she is feeling and you will be better prepared to help her. Some other important points are:

○ Model emotional regulation by labeling your own feelings out loud and how you will cope with them.

○ Teach feeling vocabulary through books by discussing the feelings the characters had and asking your child to make connections to her own experiences.

○ When you see your child experiencing an emotion, you can help her build awareness of feelings by labeling it for her. ("I noticed that when you couldn't get a cookie you tore up my papers. I am wondering if you might be frustrated, disappointed, or angry. Can you tell me more about what you are thinking about?").

○ If your child acts out when experiencing a strong emotion, label it, validate it, then provide a clear direction about what she should do instead of the negative behavior.

○ If your child is having an outburst, model calmness and use a warm, firm, and confident voice to correct the behavior.

○ Check in frequently with your child about how she is feeling. You may want to track feelings and chart them to build awareness of the connections between events, thoughts, feelings, and behaviors.

○ Teach family rules such as being safe, responsible, and respectful and remind your child of the rule when it is broken. Also, you can praise your child when she manages her emotions well and exhibits behaviors that follow the family rules.

○ Know your child's triggers or predictors for emotional or behavioral reactions. When you see a trigger, encourage a coping strategy to ward off a full-blown reaction.

○ Punishment for inappropriate behavior should be a natural consequence, not arbitrary.

○ Know your own triggers for emotional and behavioral reactions. There are always times when parents lose their cool. Being a conscious parent is not being a perfect parent. Allow yourself to make mistakes. If, out of anger or another strong emotion, you take an action or say something that you wish you hadn't, acknowledge it with your child and apologize. This will teach her to do the same, and also model how to repair a relationship when there is a conflict.

**CHAPTER 12**

Task Completion: Reaching the Finish Line

Being able to start a task is one thing, but being able to finish a task is quite another! You may find that your child starts on a number of different projects, assignments, or activities, and has trouble finishing any one of them. Or your child may begin a task and then get stuck and not know what to do. Parents can help their children and adolescents work through these difficulties by helping them understand the nature of the tasks they are expected to do and working together to find strategies for seeing tasks to completion.

What Is Task Completion?

Seeing a task to its completion, whether it is doing a chore, a homework assignment, or a long-term project, is often a challenge for children and adolescents with executive functioning weakness. As a parent, you may find yourself frustrated because your child comes to you for help the day before a big project is due and he hasn't even started it yet! Next thing you know, you are running around, getting materials for a project or staying up super late completing it with him, all the while wondering why on Earth he waited so long to start! You may also find yourself getting annoyed because simple tasks seem to take *forever* for your child to do. Parents of kids with executive functioning challenges often say, "What should take ten minutes takes hours!"

Why is it so hard for children and adolescents with executive functioning challenges to complete tasks? There can be a number of reasons. In some cases, children will find the task overwhelming and they won't even know where to start. Or they get in the middle of the task and find it to be either boring or too hard and they quit. In other cases, they aren't able to do the task, so it's better for them to look like they *don't want* to do it than to admit they *don't know how* to do it. Or, simply put, it's better to look bad than dumb. Remember that for kids, school is their job. If you aren't finishing your work, you are going to your job all day and feeling unsuccessful, which is not a good feeling. Kids also may become distracted in the middle of the task and their attention is pulled away for so long that they never return to the task.

There are a few areas that tend to be the most problematic for kids regarding task completion: finishing short-term tasks such as individual homework assignments and chores, finishing long reading assignments, and completing long-term projects.

Short-Term Tasks

Whether it's taking out the trash or finishing a math worksheet, children and adolescents with executive functioning challenges may need support in getting things done. They often don't picture the end result of the task or the positive emotion that may be attached to it ("If I take out the trash my mom will stop nagging me" or "If I just get this math worksheet finished I can go see my friends."). Instead, they tend to focus on the present negative emotion that they don't want to do it. Studies suggest that the reason for this may be partially neurological—in children with ADHD, for example, the reward centers of the brain do not get activated for boring tasks but do for exciting or interesting tasks. This is why a child with ADHD may be able to focus on an interesting craft project or a video game for hours on end but may have a very short attention span for doing a homework task she thinks is mundane. Parents will often have to provide the spark to help kids finish undesirable tasks to completion.

Dopamine and norepinephrine are neurotransmitters in the brain that send signals between nerve cells. These neurotransmitters are involved in regulating attention and the brain's response to rewards. Researchers are debating the role of these neurotransmitters in discovering a potential biological cause of ADHD.

CHORES

Giving a child a chore or two is important because it teaches responsibility and respect. Chores don't always have to be thought of as negative things one must do. Chances are, if you present chores in this way, your child will not want to do them. Frame chores as something you do to show respect for your family and pride in your responsibility. You can also tell your child that doing chores without a fuss frees up time to hang out with her friends and family, and that in the time it takes to argue about doing it, it could be done! You might start by writing up a list of all the chores that have to be done in the family, and next to each chore, have a space for filling in who does the chore. Then give your child a choice about which chores she wants to take responsibility for. Giving your child choice in chores can be helpful in ensuring they get done.

The type of chore you assign your child may also depend on the child's age. Younger children will need more explicit instruction in how to do certain chores than older children. For example, telling your six-year-old to "set the table" might not be enough instruction. You might need to walk her through it, step by step. With younger children especially, you might start by doing the chore together and then gradually give more independence. You can also try to make a game out of the chore. For example, you can give each child in your house a laundry basket, set a timer, and see how many toys they can collect in the house in five minutes. With older children, you might brainstorm ways to make chores less mundane, such as by allowing them to listen to an iPod while doing the chore. Or you can have family chore time together, setting aside time to do something fun together when you are all finished.

Doing a chore and doing a chore well are two different things! You will need to discuss the expectation of the quality of chores before asking your kids to complete them. Remember that kids with executive functioning difficulties may not be able to conjure up on their own an image of what a set table looks like or how a clean room might look. Setting quality expectations in advance will prevent you from trying to get your kid to do a chore well only to have her dig in and resist because she "already did it." Also, break up big chores into little parts. For example, when asking your child to clean her room, you might divide the chore into three parts: toys, clothes, and bed. Then, talk with your child about the subtasks: pick up your toys and put them in the toy area, put dirty clothes in the hamper, hang clean clothes up, make the bed, take items that do not belong in bed back to where they belong, etc.

Should you give your child money to complete chores? There is controversy about whether providing money for chores teaches kids that they only need to pitch in when there is something in it for them. On the other hand, parents report that money is a very powerful incentive. You can balance this out by having core chores that are done because they are a part of being in a family and extra chores your child can do for money.

After you and your child have selected her chores and discussed the quality expected, you will also need to discuss the rationale behind them.

The rationale will help you when your child balks at the chore. For example, if a bedroom is messy, then there is little room to play, and perhaps a friend cannot come over to play as a result. If you don't do laundry, you will have nothing clean to wear. If bathrooms are not cleaned, it will be embarrassing to have a friend over. Think of the rationale and then pick your chores (and battles!) accordingly. If you can't think of a valid reason your teenager should make her bed every day, it will be harder to enforce. Getting angry or becoming authoritarian about chores ("You do them because I said so!") tends to backfire.

One way to encourage responsibility in chores is to create a charting system that may be used as a way to provide rewards. Tracking chores has a number of benefits. First, it serves as a visual reminder of which chores need to be done. Second, it shows who in the family has completed their chores and how frequently each chore is done. There is less arguing about whose turn it is to do what when there is a clear expectation of each family member. You can choose to provide special rewards for daily completion of chores, or tally up the chores completed at the end of the week and each chore might count as a point your child can redeem for a reward. Rewards do not have to be things you buy. Extra TV or screen time, ten minutes of extra time before bed, or doing a special activity together can all be used as rewards.

HOMEWORK

Developing good homework habits will help with task completion. Good habits come from consistent expectations of when, where, and how homework is done in your household. Children with executive functioning challenges may need more structure than your average child to see homework to completion. They may get distracted, have difficulty getting started, get stuck, give up easily, or fail to complete the homework to the standard.

Children can start to develop homework habits as young as preschool age. In preschool, and especially the summer before kindergarten, engage your child in a sit-down activity, such as a coloring book page, at the same time each day to get him in the rhythm of having a set homework time.

TIME

You can help your child by first setting up a designated time for homework. Pay attention to your child's energy level and rhythms. Some kids absolutely need to blow off some steam and do something active when they first get home from a long day of school. Others are still in school mode and will do better if they continue working right when they get home. In general, though, the earlier homework is done, the better. You might set a goal for homework to be done before dinner, for example. With adolescents, it can be an extra challenge to get them to start on homework early. If you are seeing your teen stay up late to get work done and she is getting less than eight or nine hours of sleep, it is time to have a discussion about how you can support her in finishing homework earlier so sleep is not affected. Poor sleep will actually impair executive functioning skills, as anyone who has had a bad night's sleep can tell you!

A general rule of thumb for how long your child should be spending on homework is ten minutes per grade level. So, a first grader would spend ten minutes, and a second grader would spend around twenty minutes a night. If your child is spending substantially more time on homework than expected, schedule a meeting with your child's teacher to discuss possible modifications or adjustments.

LOCATION

Set up a work area for your child that is not distracting and encourage or enforce that homework be completed in that area. This area should be away from the television, even if it is on only as background noise. For older students, consider setting up a tech-free zone to eliminate distractions. The area should be well lit, free of clutter, and comfortable. Help your child select the place to work and create the space together. You may include a basket of items she may need, such as a calculator, ruler, stapler, and pair of scissors, as well as a visual calendar or whiteboard to track short-term and long-term assignments. Having your child or teenager help design the special area may be a fun weekend activity you can do together. This way, she feels part of the process. As adults, we have workspaces that are more and less productive for us, and the same is true for children and adolescents. They may know that being by a window is a recipe for disaster because they will get distracted, or that trying to work in their bedroom means fighting the urge to take a nap instead of doing homework. Work with your child on the features of a productive workspace.

Your child's ideal workspace may clash with your idea of an ideal workspace. The best workspace is the one that gets results—in this case, homework completed in a timely manner. Allow some flexibility of the homework space, but be sure to collect data on whether it is working and make modifications if necessary.

SCHEDULE

Making a plan about how homework time will be spent can increase task completion. Since children with executive functioning challenges frequently do not make a plan for completing tasks, you may want to spend the first few minutes of homework time making a plan together. Look at the assignments due the next day as well as upcoming tests and long-term projects together and write down the order of the tasks as well as an estimated time it might take to finish. Encourage your child to finish the toughest assignment first, since she will be the freshest. Make sure that she has some choice in the order of work, as this can be motivating. You can also add to her homework schedule some planned breaks or mini-rewards along the way. Having built-in incentives may also increase task completion. If you find your child dragging her feet on completing the tasks, encourage her to picture in her mind what it will look like and how it will feel to be finished and enjoying her break or reward.

At the end of homework time, you can help your child by reflecting on the process. Did she follow the homework plan? Did some tasks take longer than expected? Did some tasks take less time? What worked in terms of eliminating distractions? What pulled away her focus? Did she remember to complete all the parts of the assignment? Asking these questions will help your child self-monitor and make better homework plans the next time.

TRACKING PROGRESS

Having a visual representation of progress is motivating. Just think of the satisfaction you get when crossing a big to-do item off your list, or marking on your calendar that you did your workout as planned. Among the reasons people keep track of things is to see their progress and feel accomplished. You can do the same for your child by creating goal charts. First you pick a goal that is measurable and reachable. You might need to start simple and then raise the bar, so the child experiences a taste of success. You wouldn't start your goal of getting fit with "run a marathon," would you? No, you'd probably start with walking, then running, and increase the distance each time. Some sample goals to track may include:

- ☐ Start on homework right away.
- ☐ End homework before dinnertime.
- ☐ Read for twenty minutes a day.
- ☐ Work without technology interruptions for thirty minutes.
- ☐ Complete 80 percent or more of math worksheets in a week.
- ☐ Complete four out of five history journal entries in a week.

Goals should be "SMART" — **S**pecific, **M**easurable, **A**ttainable, **R**ealistic, and **T**imely. A good example might be "My child will finish homework due the next day and spend twenty minutes reading before dinnertime on four out of five evenings."

You and your child can also develop a "reward menu" for when she meets her daily or weekly goal. You can have a simple reward menu ("Meet your daily goal, get a reward") or a more complex one, in which each daily goal met is either redeemed for a small reward or saved for a larger reward ("If you meet your daily goal five times, you get a bigger reward."). These rewards do not have to be monetary or tangible, though parents can elect to go this route. You could have a special time together, or plan an activity to do as a family, or allow access to things that are off-limits until homework is done, such as having friends over, watching TV, or playing video games.

It is important to have the system be as visual as possible. Your child can help you create the chart and reward menu so she feels some owner-ship over it. There are a number of online programs that parents and children can use to create incentive charts together. Your local office-supply store may also have premade charts you can buy. Or you can get a big calendar and put a sticker on each day when your child meets her goal.

It is important to keep the tracking system positive. If you find yourself threatening to take things away instead of offering incentives for completing tasks, shift the way you talk about the system. Instead of "If you don't finish, you don't get TV" say "Think of how great it will be when you have earned the privilege of watching your favorite show when you are done" or "Do you need help finishing so you can earn TV time?"

Reading Assignments

In addition to daily homework, your child may also have assigned reading. It could be reading in a textbook, reading a novel, or doing required out-side reading of his choice. Children with executive functioning challenges may struggle with completing reading tasks on time for a variety of rea-sons. Some may underestimate how long it will take to do a reading, some will put off reading because it's not something that is technically "due" the next day, and some will have difficulties reading efficiently and remember-ing what they read. Other children will flat-out not enjoy reading, making it very challenging to motivate them to read.

READING SCHEDULES

One way to help your child break big reading assignments into smaller, more manageable parts is to help him set a reading schedule. Take the reading assignment your child has been assigned and break it down into chunks of pages he should read each night until the evaluation (whether it be a book report, quiz, test, or in-class essay). If there is a book report involved, you will need to help your child understand that the reading has to be done several days before the book report, so there is time to do the written portion as well. If your child has a planner or calendar, have your child write down the reading goal as if it were an assignment. You may want to put the reading goal on a small Post-it so if your child does not finish, he can easily move the Post-it to the next day and he will have a visual of how work can stack up if you don't do it a little at a time.

Many teachers will assign daily reading as homework. One way to help your child feel accomplished in this task is to create a reading log (if the teacher does not already provide one). For each twenty- to thirty-minute reading session, your child can mark in the log when he finishes the session. You can make these more visual and fun and weave in your child's interests as well. For example, if your child loves trains, you can add a new construction paper train car to the engine for each completed reading session and see how long you can make the train. Or if he is interested in coloring, you can buy a coloring book or download a mandala design (a circular design that can be colored) and for each reading session completed, he can color in one part of the design or picture until the entire page is colored in.

If your child is struggling with reading, you will want to consult with your child's teacher and the school psychologist about whether there is a suspicion of a reading disability. Reluctance to read can be a sign of executive functioning weakness as well as a sign of an underlying reading disorder.

If your child is resisting reading or struggling with the mechanics of reading, you might ask for support from your child's school for strategies to use at home. Some parents report that their child takes an extraordinarily long time to read, and has great difficulty completing reading in time. In this case, you might think about modifications and accommodations, such as getting a book list in advance of it being assigned (perhaps the summer before or over winter break) so your child can get started ahead of time. You might also consider downloading the audiobook version onto a personal music device or computer and have your child listen to the book while he follows along in the text to speed up the process.

Long-Term Projects

Children and adolescents with executive functioning difficulties often have a hard time working on tasks that are not due the next day. Often, teachers will break larger projects into a series of smaller tasks with due dates, and at other times, a project will be assigned and doing the smaller tasks in advance is up to the student. When there is already a breakdown of the subtasks needed in a project, it is a lot easier to support your child. For example, if your child has a science project, the teacher may have students pick an experiment by a certain date, write up a hypothesis a week later, run the experiment a few days later, turn in a rough draft of a write-up the following week, and finally create a poster for the science fair the next week. If you know in advance the subtasks involved and when they are due, you can prevent yourself from having to run out to the store to get science-experiment materials and poster board the night before and staying up late with your child to get everything done.

You can also teach your child about managing long-term projects in a fun way. You can buy any number of crafts or building toys that will teach kids how to do a little bit at a time in order to complete the final project.

One technique for helping your child take the long view in completing long-term projects is to take each step and put it on the calendar on the due date. Or, if there are no interim due dates and the project is just due at the end of the semester, then you can assign due dates based on how long you and your child think it will take to get it done. You might work backward from the due date and plan out what steps are needed and in what order. It may help to use the technique of writing the subtasks (such as "Pick a science topic" or "Write a hypothesis") on a Post-it and put it on the child's calendar or in her planner. As you check in on progress, if your child has not done the task, re-calendar all of the tasks by moving the Post-its. If your child's teacher has given a write-up of all the components of a project, you might even copy that page and actually cut out the steps to tape to a calendar or planner. You might consider using tape that can be unstuck easily in case your child falls behind in her plan.

Important Points to Consider

It can be understandably frustrating when your child fails to follow through on finishing tasks. Stop and think before reacting. The task may be too difficult, your child might not understand the parts, or he might not know where to start. If you think of staying power to finish a task as a skill to practice, like any other, you are less likely to become annoyed or angry when tasks are not seen to completion.

○ For short-term tasks, encourage your child to picture the end result of doing the task and the positive emotion that may be attached to it.

○ Present the idea of doing chores as a way to show respect for your family and pride in your responsibility. Give your children some choice in which ones they would like to be responsible for. Discuss the quality expectation of chores before asking your kids to complete them.

○ Hold consistent expectations about when, where, and how homework is done in your household.

○ Make a plan about how homework time will be spent by looking over what your child has to do that evening and what is "on-deck" and together come up with the order of the tasks and time estimations.

○ Create goal charts with your child to track success. You may build in rewards for when he reaches his goals. Rewards do not have to be purchased; they can be extension of privileges, for example.

○ Break long reading assignments into smaller, more manageable parts and make a reading schedule together.

○ For long-term projects, help your child see the long view by taking each task and putting it on a calendar with a series of interim due dates.

CHAPTER 13

Organization: Keeping Track of It All

Organization of materials is critical to school success. There is nothing more frustrating than working with your child every night on homework and then getting an e-mail from your child's teacher saying your child hasn't turned in anything for three weeks! Losing needed items, or forgetting to bring schoolwork, books, and personal items, is a source of stress for many families with children with executive functioning difficulties. Having a child with organizational challenges may be particularly stressful for parents who are highly organized. The goal isn't to turn your child into a caricature of the perfect student, but to teach him the skills he needs to be successful, while respecting that his personal organizational system may be looser than your own.

Organization Is in the Eye of the Beholder

Children with organizational difficulties are frequently messy and require more support than others their age to remember (or find!) needed items. Studies have shown that explicit instruction in organization improves organization of materials, homework management, time management, planning, and grades. The important thing to remember about teaching organization tips to your child is that you must find the strategies that work best for *your child*. Often these are not the same strategies that work for *you*. There is no "right" way to be organized. The right way is the way that works. You may be super organized and love pencil-and-paper lists (and crossing things off lists!). Your child may not respond to checklists but may respond to pictures of what she needs to remember, or she may prefer using technology, such as an application on her phone. Taking an exploratory stance will go a long way toward helping your child become organized. Present many different options and have your child experiment with them to see which ones give results, such as more homework turned in or being on time more frequently because she is not looking for lost items. It is important to consistently process what is and is not working. It must be a joint effort. Just think if someone came into your workspace and "organized" everything for you. You might find that you wouldn't know where things were, or that there was a system in place that didn't really work for you.

Finding the Floor in Your Child's Bedroom

One of the problems with a messy room is that when your child needs something, he may have a difficult time finding it. Then, when you are trying to get out the door in the morning, you'll be frantically trying to find his other shoe or the homework he finished the night before.

One way to prevent this is to follow the mantra "Everything has a home." Create a designated space for the same type of items and contain them in that space in the room every time. There may be a designated reading space where all books go, a box for stuffed animals, a crate for hard plastic toys with lots of parts, a shoe rack for shoes, and a box for art supplies. If your child does his homework in his room, then there should be a desk space with crates or a filing cabinet for all things homework-related. In general, you want most of the containers to be transparent. Traditional toy boxes or nontransparent crates are often problematic because they end up being black holes for random things your child cannot see. Children and adolescents with organizational difficulties may also profit from visual reminders of where each item's "home" is. You can take pictures of items and place them on the outside or top of the container where they belong as a visual reminder. Or for older children, you can invest in a label maker and label where things go that way.

Pinterest is a great website for finding ideas for organizing kids' spaces. Parents and professionals upload photos of ways to contain clutter, organization solutions, and creative ideas for making an organized space. Use search terms such as "kids' space organization ideas" on *www.pinterest.com* to get started.

You will also want to set specific times during the day to do a mini de-cluttering. Perhaps weekend mornings are a time to make sure everything is in its "home." You can help by picking up items and asking your child, "Where is the home for this?" You might also have a designated daily time to de-clutter, such as right before your bedtime routine. If your child's stuff tends to migrate all over the house, you can take a basket around the house, fill it up with your child's items, and help your child sort the items back into their "homes."

You may also periodically want to do a big clean-out if your child tends to be a bit of a pack rat or just has a lot of stuff. Many kids do not know how to get rid of things in a systematic way. You can speed up the process by helping him decide what is trash and what is treasure. For example, you can put out three large laundry baskets (or plastic containers) and designate them "Things to throw away," "Things to give away," and "Things to store." You might use the "Things to store" basket for toys that are not played with as much but that your child is not willing to get rid of yet. Then, periodically, you can take out the "Things to store" basket and your child can decide whether the toys are still wanted and trade out ones he hasn't played with in a while with ones that have lost their luster.

Older children and adolescents can also profit from these strategies. When you're dealing with an older child, you may be creating extra "homes" for personal items such as phones, keys, and wallets/purses. You might be contending with too many clothes strewn everywhere rather than toys, but the same system of sorting, containing, and putting them in their "homes" still applies.

Teenagers sometimes think of their own rooms as private retreats and may resent you for trying to change them. It may be developmentally appropriate for a teenager to have a messy room. It may only be necessary to intervene and help her organize if the messiness causes other problems, such as not being able to find things, or health and safety concerns.

The Backpack Vortex

There is nothing scarier than a disorganized child's backpack! You never know what you might find—lunch leftovers from two days ago, a permission slip you signed a week ago, a crumpled-up essay your child worked so hard on but forgot to turn in, dirty gym clothes, you name it! The backpack tends to be a receptacle for all things in your child's life, and for kids with organizational challenges, it can be a parent's nightmare. You might find that you can clean it out together one day and the next day it's a mess again.

The "everything has a home" technique also works for backpacks. You can designate spaces in the backpack for certain categories of items (front zipper pouch for pencils and supplies, side pockets for water bottles, front flap for homework folder, etc.).

One of the other challenges for kids with organizational issues is that they might not remember the correct textbook or book they need, or that their backpack is so cluttered it is bursting at the seams. To alleviate this problem, you might consider getting a second set of textbooks for home, so your child doesn't have to remember which textbook she needs each night—they are already there at home in her workspace.

Finally, you may also want to set a backpack-cleaning routine. For example, when your child gets home from school, you can take everything out of her backpack and help her organize it for homework time. It is important to ask your child questions about the organization rather than do it for her. You might ask, "Where is the home for your pencils?" or "What is your system for filing loose papers?" Regarding loose papers, there should be a rule that every piece of paper has a home. This prevents the crumpled-up-paper-at-the-bottom-of-the-backpack phenomenon.

Binder Systems

Continuing the theme of "everything has a home," you will want to help your child develop a system for all of his papers. The system that works best for your child will be a matter of preference. Some kids prefer to have one master three-ring notebook, or an accordion file with tabs for each subject. Other kids prefer to have one folder or binder for each subject.

Sometimes teachers have particular binder systems that they want their students to follow, and students are graded on it. In that case, you can teach your child that sometimes you have to conform to the teacher's idea of organization, even if it is not your preferred method. Frame it as a way to possibly learn a new or better way to organize.

Regardless of the system, color-coding is your friend! At the beginning of the school year, designate a color for each subject. Cover each textbook in paper that color, buy dividers or folders in that color, and you can even buy Post-its, tabs, and/or index cards in that color. This way, your child will begin to associate a color with a subject (for example, math is blue) and at the end of the school day, he can grab all the blue items if he has a math test the next day. This will keep him from grabbing the wrong folder or book.

It is worth noting that adolescents with organizational challenges often struggle with finding a home for their notes. Notes typically aren't turned in to the teacher, but they are still needed for studying. Notes can be found all over the place in a disorganized backpack—scrawled on loose pieces of paper, English notes in a science notebook, notes from multiple classes on one piece of paper, or no dates on the notes so it is hard to know what needs to be kept and what is no longer needed. Again, you will want to talk with your adolescent about a strategy that might work for him and provide a possible system for him to try (one notebook for all notes, notes in a section of each subject's folder, etc.).

There are also electronic applications for organizing notes for a research project or taking notes in class and integrating them with resources from the web or online textbooks. Notability and Evernote are examples of such applications. To get full use out of the application, your child's school will need to allow use of iPads or laptops.

Homework Systems

Children and adolescents with organizational challenges often have trouble keeping track of homework—what is due, when it is due, when and where to turn it in, etc. It only compounds the problem if your child is losing papers left and right. There is nothing more aggravating than knowing your child is not getting any credit for her hard work. It has to be frustrating for your child too!

One way to help your child develop a homework system is to create a "do-done" folder. Get a very durable plastic folder and designate the left side as the "do" side, for homework that has yet to be done. Designate the right side as the "done" side, for homework that has been completed and is ready to turn in. You can use a label maker to designate the sides or a Post-it that you seal onto the folder with clear packing tape. Encourage your child to file her assignments for all her classes in this folder during the day. After she has completed the assignments, ensure that she has put them on the "done" side. At the beginning of this process, you can enlist the help of your child's teacher(s), if possible, to check that she is putting assignments in the right side.

There will be assignments that are not worksheets, such as "Study for history quiz" or "Read Chapter 4 of your Biology text and take notes." In these cases, enlist your child in brainstorming about how to make sure these things get done. Some children like putting Post-it notes with the homework item on the "do" side. Others like putting it on an index card and putting it in the pocket. Yet others prefer to put the homework assignment in their planners for reference, and then if they have a paper product that has to be turned in, they file it on the "done" side when it is complete. There may be cases when your child has to do an assignment such as reading and taking notes, but doesn't have to actually turn anything in. In this case, help her find the "home" for reading notes, which may be in a folder or section for that particular class.

Another issue with homework systems is that there are assignments that need to be done as a part of a long-term project but aren't necessarily "due." For example, if your child has a semester-long research project, it may not make sense to put all the necessary paperwork in the "do" side of the folder. Or it may be helpful to have a separate do-done folder for the long-term project.

It is worth repeating that the best organizational system is the one that makes sense to and works for your child. You can collaborate on different systems and then evaluate how they worked—did this system increase the percentage of homework turned in? If not, then you can work with your child to determine if it wasn't properly implemented or if a new system is needed.

A big problem for children and adolescents with organizational issues related to homework is what to do with all the returned papers. Kids with executive functioning challenges do not automatically ask themselves the questions needed to decide what is trash and what is treasure. You can help your child decide by asking questions such as:

O Do you need this paper to study for a test in the future?

O Is this a paper you are proud of and want to keep?

O Do you need to keep this paper because your teacher expects you to put it in a portfolio for the end of the year?

O Is there a way we can make sure your teacher graded and recorded this piece of paper?

Asking these questions will help your child eventually ask herself the same questions to make a decision about what to keep and what to recycle. Some children get anxious about getting rid of anything until the end of the year. In this case, you can help your child by developing a filing system at home, so she can periodically move the papers from her backpack or locker to a safe place at home. It could be as simple as a crate or box where all the returned papers can go until the end of the semester or year. You could also have your child develop a "to file" folder within her backpack so that as papers are returned, they have a temporary "home." Then, your child can do a daily or weekly filing (or when the folder is too full!) so the papers don't get thrown in with active papers he needs easy access to.

Planners

The importance of using some sort of planner cannot be underscored enough! Planners are useful for keeping track of what is due, what is on-deck, and what other activities may take up time each day. Kids with organizational challenges frequently balk at the idea of a planner. This can be for a number of reasons. Some kids think that they are too much work. They often delude themselves into thinking they can keep track of everything without one. Older kids may say that they can just go on a teacher's website or text a friend to find out what is due. This works some of the time but has serious flaws. The biggest flaw in this system is the "you don't know what you don't know" phenomenon. Kids may not know to check a teacher's website or ask a friend what is due next week or when the test is. They may be shortsighted and only ask about what is due the next day. Planners are essential for helping kids project into the future and plan their time accordingly.

So how do you encourage your child to keep a planner? The answer is you must help him develop ownership over the type of planner he keeps. It doesn't matter if it is electronic or written, big or small, the one the school provides or one your child picks up at an office-supply store, as long as it has a calendar view (at minimum, a week at a glance; a month at a glance is better). Daily planners are problematic because a child can turn the page and—surprise!—a big project or big test is the next day. Online calendars for older kids are good because you can often toggle between daily, weekly, and monthly, and you can set reminders.

Younger children may be more interested in using a planner that has some creative aspect to it. They may have stickers they can put on the days of big tests, activities, or appointments. You can also extend the color-coding system you devised for each subject to the planner, where all assignments are written in the same color that was designated for the subject. Office-supply stores have multicolor pens that can easily click between colors that may be fun for your child.

Some schools prohibit the use of electronics during the school day, which may limit your child's choice in planners. Inquire with your child's teacher(s) about their policy and if appropriate, ask for an accommodation, such as supervised use of electronic planners at the end of class when homework is being assigned.

Perhaps the most important part of helping your child or adolescent with using his planner is to frequently check in about its use. As adults, we often forget that changing a habit can be difficult. People often start out with energy and excitement about a new plan, but it quickly fizzles out. Have you ever tried to make working out a daily habit? You might go to the gym every day for a few weeks, and then your energy peters out and you're back to once a month before you know it. But just think if you had a personal trainer waiting for you at the gym. You'd be a lot more likely to go! You are your child's organizational personal trainer of sorts. Until a planner becomes second nature, you may need daily check-ins and reminders, then weekly, then spot checks as needed. You may also need to enlist the help of your child's teacher(s) for support up front. If your child's teacher is on board, it would also be helpful for her to consistently check that your child is using the planner throughout the school year. The ultimate responsibility for keeping a planner is your child's, but you increase the chances of success if people in two settings are checking on it.

Helping Lost-and-Found "Frequent Flyers" Keep Track of Belongings

Have you purchased five lunchboxes for your child in one school year? Do you find yourself wondering why you buy nice jackets for your child since they never seem to make it home? Is your child a "frequent flyer" to the school's lost-and-found? Children with executive functioning challenges often misplace items or lose them altogether. They seem to lack the ability to go through a mental checklist of all the things they brought with them and all the things that need to find their way home too.

Checklists work to some degree, but the problem is that what is on a checklist may change daily. For example, some days your child does need a coat, and some days she doesn't need her soccer uniform. A checklist for core items she always needs may work, though. For example, an adolescent may always need her keys, wallet, and phone. She should be encouraged to put these three items in a "home" within your home—a bowl by the front door, a basket in her bedroom. Then, before she leaves the house, she can go to the "home" where these three items are and say to herself, "I need three things. Keys, check. Wallet, check. Phone, check."

So how do you help your child remember items that she sometimes needs and sometimes doesn't? Start with a visualization activity when your child is leaving the house. Group the items she has in big categories—clothes, school stuff, food, sports/activities stuff—and have her take a mental picture of everything she has in each of these categories. Then, at the end of the school day, remind her of the mental picture she took and ask her if she has the same items in each group. If your child is particularly forgetful (or you aren't going to remember what she brought that day), you can snap a quick picture with your phone's camera of her holding all her stuff and then at the end of the school day, show her that picture and have her double-check that she has everything. If she is missing any items, she can track them down before leaving school.

Another strategy for making sure your child doesn't leave things behind is to teach the mantra "Do the spin" after she leaves a space, such as leaving a restaurant, getting off a bus, or leaving her desk space. By spinning around before she leaves an area, she may see something she would have otherwise forgotten. Young kids especially may enjoy doing the spin because it's fun to spin around. Just make sure the child is actually looking for items and not just twirling for fun!

Important Points to Consider

Be aware of how your own organizational style may impact how you deal with your child's organizational issues. If you are super organized, you may try to impose an unrealistic expectation on your child. The best organization system is the one that works for your child, and it may take some time to come up with one that fits his needs. Be patient with your child as he tries new organizational systems. Just think of a habit you have tried to change—going to the gym more, organizing all your bills instead of putting them in a big pile, being proactive with chores—and recognize that everyone has bursts of organization and days when organization takes a backseat to other obligations. New systems take time to sink in, and they may evolve over time.

O Teach your child the mantra "Everything has a home" for remembering to put belongings in their proper place. Use this technique for backpacks as well.

O Use labels or pictures of items as visual reminders of where items belong.

O To help your child remember core items he always needs, have a "home" for these items and help your child make a short checklist of items needed every day.

O Help your child with larger de-cluttering projects by teaching him how to get rid of things in a systematic way, such as by sorting items into three baskets—throw away, give away, and store.

O For homework papers, help your child make a "do-done" folder, where he puts homework he has to do on one side and completed homework on the other.

O Encourage the use of a planner. Help your child find the planner that best suits his needs. Frequently check in to see whether your child is using his planner and, if possible, enlist the help of his teachers to check as well.

O Teach your child to "Do the spin" after he leaves a space and check for items he would have otherwise forgotten.

**CHAPTER 14**

Setting Up a Supportive Home Environment

Having structure in the home environment is essential for teaching and supporting executive functioning skills. If your home tends to be chaotic, unpredictable, and disorganized, your child will adapt to that environment and mimic the disorganization. If your home is calm, positive, predictable, and structured, your child will have a better chance of learning how to regulate her own behavior and implement strategies for success. Being a conscious parent is not the same as being a perfect parent. Don't judge yourself harshly if your home is somewhat disorganized. Instead, reflect on a few areas for improvement that may create more harmony in the household and take an experimental approach to making changes.

Making the Home Environment Positive for Teaching Executive Functioning

One feature of a positive home environment is the type of feedback that a child receives. It can be easy to get stuck in a nagging cycle with your child, and as a result, most of the feedback he gets is corrective, not positive. This is akin to you going to your job every day and your boss only noticing your work when you make an error, constantly reminding you not to make an error, and getting exasperated with you when you do make an error. This type of feedback is not particularly motivating, or it is motiving to a degree but uncomfortable because you are motivated by fear or by not failing rather than by feeling successful and proud of the things you are doing well.

A good rule of thumb is that feedback to your child about his behavior should follow the "3-S rule":

O **Specific:** Instead of saying "good job," be specific. Say "I like how you double-checked to see that you had your permission slip" or "I noticed you used your words to tell me you were frustrated instead of throwing things. Thank you!" This way, your child will know exactly what he did that was appreciated.

O **Sincere:** Kids can see through a fake compliment easily. Don't spout off compliments that are not true, or add any layer of sarcasm to the compliment. If you are having trouble finding something positive to comment on, look deeper. Your child may have successfully completed part of a task ("You did a great job setting up your desk for homework time. May I help you get started now?") or may have put in effort, even if you haven't seen the results you are looking for yet ("I see you are trying to keep up with using your planner.").

O **Sporadic:** Praise that is handed out all the time loses its value. The best time to give specific praise is when your child is first learning a skill. Once he has mastered the skill, a compliment every now and then to show you still appreciate the positive behavior will motivate your child to continue.

Another feature of a positive home environment is having a multi-sensory learning environment. This means that you are combining visual, verbal, and kinesthetic modalities when you are trying to teach your child how to do a task that involves executive functioning. Having visuals such as charts, calendars, checklists, pictures, and labels can help to remind your child what is expected. Parents should also verbally mediate their thought processes and the steps they take when doing tasks. This means talk out loud when you are doing a task that requires planning, organizing, and the like. Your child is learning from watching and listening to you. The more you can discuss the rationale behind strategies you are using, the more likely your child will buy into them as well. Be explicit when you are teaching a skill, because if your child knew these things implicitly, he would likely be doing them already.

Routines and consistency are the final ingredients for setting up a successful home environment. You may need to collaborate with other family members about the routines that will work for everyone in the family. The more predictable your child's home life is, the better. Of course, you will also be teaching how to cope with changes in routines, but in general, having routines gives a child an external structure for his days, since his internal structure is not developed enough yet to cope with his multiple responsibilities.

Routines Are Your Friends!

Routines are important because they give your child a sense of control, and they can reduce anxiety because the child knows what is going to happen. We often forget what it is like to be a kid. Imagine if someone didn't explain why you had to do something, or sprang things on you without warning. Imagine you were put in a car and not told where you were going, how long you'd be gone, or when you'd return. It would be fairly anxiety-provoking! Routines are especially important for children and adolescents who lack internal structure because of executive functioning weaknesses. So how do you build routines into your family's home life?

First, identify the routine that you want to start with. Start with one routine and build from there. Enlist your child in a discussion of how you envision the routine going and see if you can get her on board with improving it. Say something like, "In the mornings, I notice we are often late, and I end up yelling at you to get moving. I don't like yelling at you and I'm sure we can find a way together to have a smooth morning. Let's start by creating a routine together." This way, you are operating as a team and you have explained the rationale. If you skip this step, your child may think you are trying to impose rules on her for no good reason. If you already have a routine but it is not working well, engage your child in problem-solving about why it is not working. In general, you will want to have a solid routine for the following times:

O **Morning routine:** get up, make bed, get dressed, brush hair, eat breakfast, gather materials for the day, brush teeth

O **Return-from-school routine:** put book bag and belongings in their "homes," get snack, play for fifteen minutes, begin homework

O **Homework routine:** gather needed materials, set up desk, eliminate distractions, set homework plan with parent, start on hardest task first, take break, finish easy tasks, do required reading, earn reward/free time

O **Dinner routine:** stop and put away current activity, wash hands, help set table, eat, clear table

O **Bedtime routine:** take bath, put on pajamas, brush teeth, read book, lights out

It is important to note that some kids will need transition prompts or warnings before each routine. Saying something like, "In ten minutes we are going to start our bedtime routine" will give your child a chance to prepare for the transition. Some children will need you to walk them through the steps one at a time. Other kids will need added visual support to make the transition. You can have pictures or a list of the tasks within each routine and ask, "What is next?" It's easier to argue with a parent than with a list, so this can be a useful strategy for kids who are resistant to following the routine.

Stop the Homework Battles

There is nothing worse than spending your afternoon or evening battling with your child or teen about homework. You may feel like a nag, he may feel that you're overbearing, and it's hard on the relationship. The ultimate goal is to make homework time a more pleasant experience for everyone involved. The first step is to evaluate why it's a battle in the first place. Is the homework too easy? Too hard? Too long? Not stimulating? Overwhelming? Okay for some subjects or tasks but not for others? The intervention will vary depending on the reason homework is a struggle for your child. Talk with your child about the thoughts and feelings he has about homework. Some children may just say, "It's boring" or "I don't like it." Your job is to delve further ("What parts are boring?" "Are there any parts that aren't boring?" "What parts don't you like?" "Are there parts you do like?"). Ask your child's teacher if she observes resistance to certain subjects or tasks. Inquire about your child's skill level in each subject and ensure that failure to complete tasks is not due to lack of understanding.

> The research on how effective homework is for increasing learning and achievement is mixed. Some studies show a positive correlation and others show negative correlations. Yet others show that too much homework can actually be detrimental to learning. A recent analysis of 100 studies on homework showed the strongest positive correlation between homework and learning at the high-school level.

It is also important to have a discussion with your child about the rationale behind homework. Homework serves to strengthen or extend the skills learned at school, teaches responsibility, and perhaps most importantly, gives the teacher feedback about what concepts are solid and what else needs to be taught. When you frame homework as information for the teacher, your child may be more responsive and less defensive than if you present it as a necessary evil in his life. By saying, "This will show your teacher what you know and what you need to know," you take the pressure off having to do it perfectly. As a parent, it is so tempting to ensure your child gets all his work done by helping a lot or even resorting to practically doing it for him. Just think of the big picture. If you give too much help, you are denying your child's teacher valuable information, such as that your child needs extra support at school to master the content.

Be careful not to project your own negative feelings about homework onto your child. When you frame homework as a negative chore to be done, chances are that is exactly how your child will see it. If you can find a kernel of positivity about homework (teaching responsibility, reinforcing skills, or learning something interesting), your child will likely be more positive as well.

Sometimes kids who seek a lot of attention from you during homework time may actually be seeking connection. Instead of thinking he should just be independent, think about homework time as a way to connect to your child. Learn what he is learning about and you can have interesting discussions together. Work through difficult tasks together and your child will view you as a supportive person in his life. Some parents will choose work they have to do and simply sit next to their child while he does homework. This can send an implicit message that everyone has work to do, and it can be more pleasurable when you have a work companion.

There are times, of course, when the dynamic between you and your child around homework is so negative that you reach a point of no return. Perhaps after years of sitting next to your child and walking through every step of homework, you have grown weary and your child is annoyed by your presence, as it is a daily reminder that he can't do it on his own. Some parents elect to remove themselves from the equation and enlist the support of another person. Parents may hire a tutor, coach, teacher, older peer/sibling, or an educational therapist to work with their child a few times a week to ease the tension in the parent-child relationship. Ask your child's school what resources are available. There may be an afterschool program, free peer tutors, or a study hall where your child can receive one-on-one or small-group support. If you have the financial means, you can also ask for referrals for professional tutors or educational therapists to come to your home and support the homework routine.

An educational therapist is a trained professional who provides a variety of specialized services for children with learning differences. You can find an educational therapist in your area by visiting the Association of Educational Therapists online at *www.aetonline.org*.

It is worth noting that children with executive functioning challenges may also be diagnosed with a learning disability, an autism spectrum disorder, or attention deficit hyperactivity disorder and may need modified homework. Some teachers will give shortened or different homework assignments tailored to their ability level or interests, so that students are more successful in completing them. Some schools will provide these accommodations in the general education environment, and others will require that your child be officially in special education or have a 504 accommodation plan in place to offer these modifications. Inquire with your child's teacher, the principal, or the school psychologist for more information.

A 504 plan refers to Section 504 of the Rehabilitation Act and Title II of the Americans with Disabilities Act. These laws require schools to make special accommodations for students with disabilities in order for them to perform at the same level as their peers. More information can be found at *www2 .ed.gov/about/offices/list/ocr/504faq.html*.

Getting Your Child to Do Chores

If you are wondering why your child won't just do her chores, think about why *you* don't like to do chores. Same reason! Chores are typically boring or there's usually something more fun you'd rather be doing. You end up doing them out of necessity, but for a kid, it's hard to think of a necessary reason she should stop playing to do something undesirable. There are supports you can put in place at home that can increase the chance of your child doing chores.

Timing is everything. Chances are, if you catch your child at a moment when she is doing something fun and you ask her to do her chores, she will say, "I'll do it later!" and you may or may not see her finish the chore. You can build chores into your daily routine, so that chores happen before fun. It's much easier to motivate your child to do a chore when she knows fun is on the horizon. You can also allow a little bit of flexibility in the timing, such as giving a time window in which chores need to be done and then point out what your child will be allowed to do after ("Sometime in the next half hour the trash needs to be taken out. After it's taken out you can have screen time."). This way, it's somewhat up to your child when the chore gets done, and she learns that the faster she does it, the faster she can do what she would rather be doing.

Children and adolescents with executive functioning challenges may need added incentives to complete chores. Gaining access to a desired activity is a great motivator. Others may include special time with a parent, having a friend over, or going to bed a little later than usual. Older children may be motivated by an allowance, which they earn if they complete their daily chores. Depending on your comfort level with paying for chores, this may be an option for your family.

You may need to have a visual reminder or checklist in a common room so your child can see what needs to be done and how frequently the goal is being met. There are many chore charts you can download from the Internet, or you can create your own. You can also build in a little variety by having your child pick from a short "menu" of chores. As an adult, you know that some days, vacuuming seems like a horrible task but you don't mind doing the dishes, and on other days, the reverse is true. Your child may be more in the mood to do a certain chore, and as long as one of the designated chores is done, that may be a way to increase chore compliance.

Important Points to Consider

Don't worry or judge yourself harshly if your home is not perfectly organized and structured. Reflect on a few areas you might be willing to change to set the stage for success for your child and experiment with them. For example, pick one routine that you would like to have run smoother and work on that, instead of trying to take on several at a time. Just as you try to be patient with your children when they try things in a new way, be patient with yourself as you try to make changes.

O The building blocks for a home environment that supports children with executive functioning challenges are structure, routines, and predictability.

O Children and adolescents profit from positive discipline practices in the home. Focusing on what they are doing well goes a long way. Energy flows where your attention goes—if you focus on the positive, your child tends to do more of the positive behavior.

O Collaborate with your child on developing homework and chore routines. The more you work with your child on how to get things done in a timely manner, the better chances you have for behavioral change. Soliciting your child's input can increase buy-in for new ways to do things at home.

 **CHAPTER 15**

Parenting Children with Executive Functioning Challenges

Parenting any child has its ups and downs. Parenting a child with executive functioning difficulties—a child who needs to be taught and retaught skills that seem basic—can have even more ups and downs. There are bound to be some days when you lose your cool, and some days when you should probably get a medal for all your skillful parenting and patience! Knowing that ups and downs are a normal part of parenting a child with special needs helps during the low times. The phrase "This too shall pass" helps parents in times of frustration, because it serves as a reminder that everything, good and bad, is a phase in your child's life. You may also find it helpful to think about the role you want to have in your child's life when it comes to supporting him in developing executive functioning skills.

Your Changing Role

As a parent of a child with executive functioning difficulties, you may find yourself wearing many hats. One day, you may be encouraging your child not to give up on a difficult math assignment. The next day, you might be facilitating an extra tutorial for her. The following day, you might be stepping back and letting your child finish her work independently. The type of support you provide to your child will also change over time, as her developmental needs change. For example, you will not be sitting down next to your tenth grader doing homework in the same way you would a first grader (hopefully!). It can be difficult for some parents to know exactly what their role is in working with their child with executive functioning challenges. In general, there are several roles a parent can assume, each one appropriate at a different stage in your child's life.

Parent As Orchestrator

Early on in your child's school life, you may be a master orchestrator. Like a conductor of an orchestra, you are coordinating all the different parts of your child's life—school, home life, sports, appointments, and extra activities. You take care of his daily schedule and plan ahead for special events and big assignments at school. Your child relies on you for time management, organization, and other executive functions.

You also orchestrate nearly all of his interactions with others—friends, family members, and school peers. You make sure that he has play dates with friends and sign him up for social activities. You foster interests he may have, and also encourage him to try new things. You may coordinate special services for him as well—additional tutoring, coaching, and therapies. As the conductor of the orchestra, you are the one responsible for making sure he is where he needs to be and is doing what he needs to be doing.

Within this role, you are also teaching him skills that you hope one day he will do independently. You recognize that he is not able to perform these higher-level organizational skills just yet. You tend to teach your child by demonstrating and modeling how to do things, and then giving him a smaller step or part of the task. For example, when orchestrating a play date, you don't hand your phone to your eight-year-old and tell him to make the plans. You look at the calendar for free time, ask your child to think of a child he would like to play with, look up the parent's contact information, and call or e-mail to set the date. You coordinate the time and location. Your child's role in this process may be in giving input about who, what, when, or where. But you can teach him how to make a play date by talking through the process and reminding him of the sequence of events. This is called guided instruction because you are guiding your child through the process but he isn't expected to be very independent yet. Your role as an orchestrator may be ongoing on some level throughout your child's school career, since you will always be guiding him in learning new tasks. However, this role tends to be predominant during the preschool and elementary school years. The more severe your child's executive functioning challenges are, the longer you might stay in this role.

Parent As Monitor

As children develop, your role may change from an orchestrator to a monitor. This does not suggest that your child is left to her own devices and you just check in on her from time to time. Good monitoring also has an element of guided instruction, as well as independent practice and checking.

There is a difference between cueing/prompting and nagging. The difference is in the tone. Cueing/prompting is giving your child a heads-up about what you expect him to do in a clear and neutral tone. Nagging has a tone of exasperation and possibly anger. Nagging doesn't work very well. Just think of when your child nags you to buy a toy at the store. It doesn't make you want to buy the toy, does it?

For example, if your child is expected to clean her room, you don't just ask her to clean it and then come back and check. You start the process by prompting or cuing her. You might cue her by giving her a hint about what needs to be done ("When you clean your room, there are three zones to clean. Do you remember them?"). If this is not sufficient, you may need to give a prompt including step-by-step instruction ("When you clean your room, start with the clothing zone by putting dirty clothes in the hamper."). You may need to start with prompts if your child does not respond to cues.

Once your child has mastered a task, you can fade the cues and prompts. You may only need to give one direction ("Please clean your room") and then you can check that she did it to the standard. If she did not, then you can go back to cues ("I see you cleaned the clothes and toys zones nicely! Did you forget a zone?") or prompts ("I like how the clothes and toys zones are so neat and tidy. Let's work on the bed zone now."). It is important to praise successive approximations toward the goal so the child is encouraged to continue. Just think if you made a goal to go to the gym five days a week but you only went four times and your personal trainer chastised you for not going on the fifth day. It would be far more motivating if he praised you for going four times, right? Don't forget to praise effort toward the goal.

It is important that monitoring be done with warmth. Monitoring without warmth (the authoritarian style of parenting) has been shown to have more negative outcomes than monitoring that is perceived by the child to come from a place of caring. Reassure your child that you are checking in not because you don't trust him but because you care that he does well and feels proud of his work.

Your role as monitor is probably most prominent during homework time. Instead of having to sit next to your child the whole time, you might just need to set her up with a homework plan (what she will do first and how long she plans to spend on each task), and then pop in from time to time to check on progress. You may need to redirect your child to get back on-task, see how far she has come in her homework plan, or check to make sure she is doing the assignment correctly. You might also check in at the very end of the homework process and help your child evaluate whether everything is done and if it is done to the standard. Finally, you can support any organization system she may have, such as ensuring she puts her finished homework in the "done" side of her homework folder.

Parents of children with executive functioning challenges may be in the monitoring role longer than they had anticipated. Typically, monitoring fades in middle school, and the child is much more independent in completing tasks such as homework and projects. However, if your child struggles with executive functioning tasks such as initiating and sustaining effort, memory, and self-regulation, then fading the monitoring too early can be detrimental. There are some researchers who state that children with executive functioning problems, such as children with ADHD, function two to three grade levels behind their peers in executive functioning tasks. Thus, a child who is a sixth grader may need the monitoring and support more typical of a third or fourth grader. This means that you may have to extend your monitoring of schoolwork into the early high-school years. Of course, how long you monitor is highly dependent on the nature of your child's difficulties.

By middle school, some children will start to resent monitoring and it can be a strain on your relationship with your child. You might want to consider finding resources to take the monitoring role off your plate, such as a study-skills tutor, an older peer, study hall/afterschool tutoring programs, or an educational therapist.

Parent As Facilitator/Supporter

Once your child has some independence in completing tasks such as chores and schoolwork, you can serve as a facilitator. In this role, you do not check in as frequently as you did when you were in the monitoring role. Instead, you take advantage of opportunities to support your child and facilitate positive outcomes. For example, if your child seems to be struggling with an assignment, such as reading a novel for English class, you can offer your support. Ask your child if he would like to explore some alternative ways to get the reading done, such as downloading the audiobook to listen to in the car together, or purchasing SparkNotes or CliffsNotes so he can get the general idea of the novel before he reads it or check his understanding along the way. Your role is to generate possible solutions for your child's problem and facilitate getting the resources he may need.

Many high schools now have websites where you can check your child's grades at any time. This can be a great tool or a source of conflict between you and your teenager, depending on how it is used. If you are in the monitoring phase, you will likely check it frequently. If you are in the supporting phase, you might check periodically, or ask your child if it is okay to check it. Be sure that you are giving the message that you check because you want to provide support if needed.

You may also find yourself facilitating and supporting your child only in certain classes, and having to do more monitoring in others. Your child may be independent in his English and history classes but struggling in his math and science classes. You might seek out extra tutoring, or encourage him to see his teachers during office hours. Instead of e-mailing the teachers yourself to ask what assignments are missing, when the next big test is, or what your child's current grade is, you encourage your child to do so on his own. You might help him revise a draft of an e-mail if he has trouble getting started, but in general, your child is doing most of the work. You are like his coach, giving him tips and pointers for how to do something a little better.

Manager or Micromanager?

Conflict can arise when there is a developmental mismatch between your role and your child's development. While young children will likely have less of an issue with you orchestrating and monitoring, an older child may find it intrusive and overbearing. This is because older children are in a developmental stage where they are striving for independence. Constant prompting, reminding, and checking from parents may be an unpleasant reminder to your older child that she is dependent. She wants to do things for herself, even if it means failing at some things. This can create tension in a relationship, because parents may fear that giving their child more independence will result in disastrous consequences. Children striving for independence may show oppositional behavior or resentment or develop a sense of learned helplessness, meaning they don't do anything because they know that Mom or Dad will solve problems for them.

Helicopter Parenting

The term *helicopter parenting* has been used to describe an unhealthy dynamic of parents providing too much help to their children. This type of parenting is characterized by extreme over-parenting, such as constant e-mailing of teachers, arguing about grades on behalf of your child, calling and texting all day to remind your child of obligations, signing your child up for dozens of activities he doesn't want to do but look good on college applications, offering advice for practically everything your child does, doing his homework and projects for him, never letting him out of your sight even when he is old enough to be unsupervised, and hovering over your child and rescuing him whenever he is about to make a mistake. While intentions may seem good, research shows that this type of parenting often stems from anxiety and regret about goals the parent could not fulfill in her own life.

Asserting independence occurs at many different stages of development. At each stage, it may look different, but the core feature is that children want to be proud of their own accomplishments. Knowing that your child's desires for independence are normal can help parents understand why she may resist your offers of help.

Research also shows that there are some detrimental effects of helicopter parenting on children. If a parent is overbearing and overprotective, children may lose out on the learning opportunities that come from failure. Any parent wants to help her child avoid the discomfort of failure, but this intervention exacts a cost. It deprives the child of learning problem-solving and coping skills. Research is showing that children of helicopter parents are more likely as young adults to be anxious and narcissistic, and have trouble coping with the demands of everyday life.

No parent sets out to be a helicopter parent. Helping your child is an instinct. The problem for parents of children with executive functioning difficulties is that these children often legitimately need more help than other children. Children develop responsibility and independence at different rates, and it can be difficult for parents to know when is the right time to back off and when intervention is necessary. In general, research is showing that there are three questions you must ask yourself before providing help.

DOES MY CHILD CLEARLY NEED HELP?

The first step in determining if your child needs help is to ask him! Parents often interpret when their children need help, and in reality, they don't always need it. Of course, there are children who are reluctant to say they need help, but it is a good place to start. Next, you will want to think about what might happen if you do not provide help. Be realistic. What would really happen if he didn't finish his homework? Chances are, he would get marked down in his grade, but would it be a huge problem? The answer is: it depends. Is this a habitual pattern of not turning things in, or is it an every-once-in-a-while problem? If it is habitual, then you will want to set up a system to support him. If it is an occasional problem, then perhaps it is okay to let him have the negative consequence of telling his teacher he didn't finish his work.

If your child shows a habitual pattern of not turning in work and refusing help from you, solicit advice from your child's teacher or teachers to develop a plan. There may be resources available at school that can support your child.

IS MY HELP COMPLEMENTING MY CHILD'S EFFORT OR REPLACING IT?

When your child is experiencing a difficulty, such as finishing that science project, you might be tempted to grab the glue stick and get to work just to get it done. Unfortunately, this jumping-in sends an unintentional message that your child is not competent. In order for children to be happy, they need to feel competent and connected to others. Doing your child's work for him potentially undermines both of these criteria, since he may resent you for taking over. Asking yourself if your help is complementary or replacing your child's effort will help keep things in check. One way to provide help without taking over is to ask your child, "Is there anything that I can do to help?" and then listen to what he might find helpful. He may report that there is nothing you can do, and even if you don't believe this to be true, take it at face value. Then, if he ends up failing as a result, you can process it with him by asking questions such as, "Is there a way we could have prevented this?" or "If this project were a movie, where could we rewind it to in order to change the outcome?" This helps build coping skills for the next time a project comes around.

IS MY CHILD COMFORTABLE WITH RECEIVING HELP?

There may also be cases where your child is not comfortable receiving help, and that is perfectly fine. He may want to do things his way, and he will figure out if his way works or doesn't work in due time. If his way works, then he will have built some independence and self-confidence. If his way doesn't work, then you will have a teachable moment on your hands. For example, perhaps your child thinks he can remember all his assignments without using a planner. You offer to help him keep track of his assignments and he says he doesn't want your help because he doesn't need to use the planner. Instead of pushing your help onto him, you can say something like, "That is an interesting idea. Let's test out your theory for two weeks. If you can remember everything without writing it down, that is great. If I check with your teacher and there are missing assignments, then we will need to come up with a new strategy together." That way, you are giving him a chance to try a strategy on his own but are still making it clear that he will need to accept your help if his strategy doesn't work.

Lending Your Child Your Frontal Lobe

Knowing when and how much support and help is needed and what your role should be with your child's schoolwork and social life can be challenging. This challenge is compounded when your child also has executive functioning difficulties, because there is often a lag in your child demonstrating independent learning and social skills. This creates situations where you might be intervening more than she would like you to, because perhaps her friends' parents are more hands-off.

In essence, when you are helping your child learn executive functioning skills such as planning, organizing, paying attention, self-regulating learning tasks and emotions, maintaining control, and strengthening memory skills you are lending her your frontal lobe. Remember that the frontal lobe is the central executive in the brain that tells us what to do and how to do it. You lend your child your frontal lobe every time you talk through what should be done, cue or prompt her to complete a task, or walk her, step by step, through a complicated task.

The idea of lending your frontal lobe to your child means just that— it is on *loan*. This means that you have to provide opportunities for your child to learn because you cannot continue to be your child's frontal lobe forever. She cannot take you with her to college or into the workplace and have you plan out her day and solve all her problems for her. While parents know this intuitively, there are times when it is good to remind themselves that sometimes it is better to lose a battle than lose a war. You might need to ask yourself, "Is this help I am giving also teaching her a life skill?" and "If I don't give this help, will that help her learn in the long run?"

How to Pull Back Support Without the Crash and Burn

It is so hard to know when it's the right time to step back and let your child try tasks on his own. You may have already had an experience when you stopped monitoring and guiding your child to see what would happen and the results were not good. Perhaps you decided that you would back off helping your child track missing assignments because he said he wanted to be independent, and the number of missing assignments increased. Or maybe you decided to let your child suffer the consequences of not remembering his homework, and his grades plummeted but his behavior didn't change in the least.

The concept of "scaffolding" may be useful for understanding how to fade support in a way that doesn't create a crash-and-burn situation. When one is building a house, the first thing that is built is a foundation. For the child with executive functioning challenges, that foundation is you! You provide the basic skills that your child needs to have—controlling impulses, developing internal routines, learning how to problem-solve and cope with challenges—all by parenting your child every day. Teachers also provide a foundation, or perhaps support beams, in that they teach basic academic skills and foster social skills in the school environment.

Your child's teachers are also good resources for helping you decide when and how to pull back support. With your child's permission, you might contact the teachers and talk about a plan to fade your support. It is important to include your child in the process and the ultimate plan, so she knows what the new expectations will be and what will happen if she fails to meet those expectations.

In order to build a house to completion, though, one must use scaffolds. These are temporary structures that are designed to support the construction. In learning situations, scaffolding is the process of supporting the child until the learning is strong enough to stand on its own. The key in this metaphor is that the supports for the skills are *temporary*. However, you don't want to pull back the scaffolds until the child has the skills. Doing so would lead to a crumbling of everything that has been built. Your job as a parent is to step back and look at the big picture. Are you providing the correct scaffolds? Are you teaching your child skills or doing them for him? What would happen if you pulled back support? Can support be pulled back in one area but remain in place in others? Is there a plan for fading support? Can your child's teachers provide advice about when and how to pull back support? Asking yourself these questions will help guide you about when and how to give your child more opportunities for independence.

After High School: College and Beyond

You may have heard horror stories of helicopter parents calling their child's college professors and trying to negotiate better grades for their child, or kids who get to college and fall apart because they aren't equipped to make any decisions on their own. If your child is college-bound, then you will need to think strategically about the skills she will need once she leaves the house for the "real world." If your child is not college-bound, you will need to think about the skills needed to be a functioning adult in the workplace. The following is a list of things young adults need to be able to do after high school:

- ☐ Set an alarm and get up on time
- ☐ Keep track of appointments and changes in schedule, and maintain a calendar of events and obligations
- ☐ Follow a schedule and be adaptable when schedule changes occur
- ☐ Keep track of money—incoming, outgoing, cash flow, when bills are due—and establish a system for saving money and avoiding debt
- ☐ Keep a clean apartment or house, or contribute to chores if sharing a space with others
- ☐ Do laundry and cook meals
- ☐ Get enough sleep every night
- ☐ If in college, make choices about coursework, manage multiple subjects and professor expectations, and complete work to the standard on time
- ☐ If in the workplace, apply for a job, arrive on time, and work to the standard
- ☐ Develop new friendships while maintaining old friendships
- ☐ Build a new support network

- [ ] Navigate the dating world
- [ ] Make good use of free time, and avoid dangerous or illegal activities

---

Only 55 percent of college students graduate with diplomas, according to the National Center for Education Statistics. The United States ranks ninth in college enrollment among industrial nations but last in completion rates.

Your child may be under the impression that once she gets to college or into the work world, she will automatically step up to the task of being responsible. This may be the case, but it is not the typical case. One of the best predictors of future behavior is past behavior, and old habits can die hard. If your child is chronically late as a teen, the odds of her turning over a new leaf when she gets to college and being on time all the time are slim. So how do you encourage your child to build these young-adult skills while she is still home?

As you look at the previous checklist, pick three life skills that you want your child to have on the day she sets out to start her young-adult life. Talk about these three skills with your child and explain why you have chosen them as important. See if she also endorses these skills as important, and together make a plan for how you will foster them. It may help your child to understand why you keep after her about being on time when she sees the life skills needed to be a successful adult.

Important Points to Consider

Conscious parents reflect on their own areas of strength and need. Don't judge yourself harshly if you lose your patience or become angry with your child. Parenting a child with executive functioning difficulties can be trying, even for the most patient of people. Instead of focusing on your mistakes, make a conscious effort to forgive yourself and learn from your parenting mishaps.

O Recognize that your role shifts based on your child's age and developmental needs. Don't be concerned if you are in a different role than other parents. You are giving your child what he needs at this point in his life.

O As you decide how much to support your child with executive functioning skills, ask yourself, "Am I helping him learn a new skill?" If the answer is no, then chances are you are prioritizing a short-term gain of getting him to a goal, but losing sight of the long-term gain of teaching him how to reach his goals independently.

O The balance in deciding how much support to give and when to let your child experience failure is delicate, and sometimes it is difficult for parents. Keep the lines of communication open with your child about which task he needs support in, and which task he would like to try on his own.

CHAPTER 16

Building Resilience

As children advance in age and grade, they are expected to be increasingly independent. Your job as a parent is to advocate for your child and help her receive all the school supports she needs to be successful. However, there comes a point at which you need to also teach your child to self-advocate. Think of the day your child leaves for college. Imagine all the skills you want her to have. You can't follow your kid to college to make sure she is getting enough sleep, is not procrastinating, is being proactive in her studies, or is managing setbacks well. You can only prepare her as much as possible while she is under your roof. This is why it is so essential to build resilience skills.

Smoothing Out the Ocean versus Riding the Waves

What is resilience? Resilience is the ability to bounce back from adversity. If there are two children with equal difficulties in executive functioning and one manages to be successful despite his challenges, he is demonstrating resilience. It is important to understand which traits foster resilience and how you can promote them.

To use a metaphor, you cannot smooth out the ocean for your child throughout his whole life. You will need to give him tools to handle the waves that may come his way. A combination of external support and personal responsibility is the goal for your child. There are situations when a parent's good intentions to make things easier for a child backfire because the child becomes overly dependent on the parent. It can also be the case that parents try to get the school environment to be a "smoothed ocean" and relentlessly advocate for all kinds of changes in the school. Of course, you want to advocate for appropriate accommodations and supports, but you also need to be realistic about what the school can provide. There is value in holding your child accountable for his learning and behavior as well. Striking the balance to find the right level of support can be challenging, and it is important to keep the concept of resilience in your mind when you are trying to find this balance.

Success Factors

In order to set the stage for your child to be resilient, you will want to know the traits that are associated with success despite learning challenges. There is a growing body of research that suggests that certain character traits can be more predictive of academic success than intelligence, which has historically been the number-one predictor. The good news is that parents and teachers can help develop these success traits. It's not an all-or-nothing proposition, in which some kids are born with personality traits that help learning and some are not. The fact is, if you can change a child's mindset about her challenges, then you can see progress toward overcoming them.

SELF-AWARENESS

Self-advocacy and resilience start with self-awareness. You will want to help educate your child about the nature of her challenges so she has an understanding that she may have to work harder than other children in certain areas. The more self-aware she is about her learning and behavioral strengths and weaknesses, the better equipped she will be to ask for help, be proactive, and seek out needed resources. Have frequent conversations with your child about how every child learns differently and has her own areas where she is strong and areas where she needs to work harder. Talk about your own challenges to bring home the message. Look online for profiles of famous people with disabilities or challenges and discuss their resiliency. The more you and your child know about her challenges and ways to overcome them, the more comfortable she will feel seeking the help she needs.

The Frostig Center has a guide for parents about "success attributes" as well as practical tips for supporting your child's resilience at http://frostig.org/our-research/ld-success-predictors/.

PERSISTENCE AND GRIT

Research in the psychology of learning is burgeoning in the field of positive psychology. This means that instead of studying all the things that can go wrong in learning and development, studies are focused on positive traits that help people learn and grow in almost any circumstance. One such trait is optimism. Optimistic people tend to recover quickly from setbacks, live longer and happier lives, and embrace challenges rather than avoid them. Having positive well-being allows for more positive learning opportunities and more satisfaction.

Within the positive-psychology movement, there are certain traits that are particularly related to school success. Researcher Angela Duckworth studies the effects of persistence and motivation to succeed, a trait she calls "grit." Students with grit stick with goals over long periods of time, even in the face of failure and adversity. They have an overwhelming stamina to reach their goals and do not give up. Studies have found grit to be more important than intelligence in predicting school achievement and finishing college. This means that even with learning and executive functioning challenges, children and adolescents with grit can succeed. They just can't give up on themselves.

Your child can take the Grit Scale to gauge perseverance and passion for achieving goals at *https://sites.sas.upenn.edu/ duckworth/pages/research.*

EMOTIONAL SUPPORT

Having executive functioning difficulties is frustrating because even despite best efforts, there is room for failure. Children and adolescents who overcome failure, in addition to having personality traits such as grit, also make use of support systems. Asking for and accepting help is one of the most important traits for academic success. Kids who reach out to teachers and take advantage of office hours, tutorials, and extra help from parents and professionals are more likely to succeed. This means that your child needs to understand that asking for help is okay, and that smart kids ask for help. Encourage your child to make use of the supports available to her.

Another way to promote positive outcomes is by seeking help to manage emotional reactions to challenges and failures. Children who have at least one supportive adult in their lives tend to do better on all kinds of life outcomes—school, work, relationships, etc. The more supportive the adults in their lives, the better. Coping with learning and executive functioning challenges is not easy, and being able to talk with someone about how to cope can be very helpful. This person does not need to be a trained therapist, just a supportive, nonjudgmental, and encouraging individual. Of course, some children and adolescents can benefit from a therapeutic professional as well. If you think of a challenge you had in your life and how you overcame it, you will probably think of several people who helped you get through it. Children and adolescents need emotional support just as much as, if not more than, adults, since they may not have the skills to process and understand their challenges. They may just feel like a "bad kid" or "stupid." They may not have a toolkit of coping strategies to use in difficult times, so parents and other caring adults serve an important role in providing these tools.

You can learn more about positive psychology and the study of happiness at the University of Pennsylvania's Authentic Happiness website at *www.authentichappiness.sas.upenn.edu.* You and your child can take surveys to find out your core strengths and learn ways to integrate these strengths into your day for positive outcomes.

MINDSET

Having a growth mindset is one of the best ways to be successful and to avoid the pitfalls of perfectionism. Researcher Carol Dweck showed in a number of studies that the way you think about your abilities affects your actual performance. She divides these mindsets into "growth" and "fixed." A growth mindset is based on the belief that talents can be developed and that great abilities are built over time. It allows room for, and in fact emphasizes, the idea that mistakes are inherent in learning. Perfectionists tend to have a fixed mindset and believe that talents and abilities are set in stone—either you have them or you don't. In that case, you have to prove things to yourself over and over again, and are constantly trying to look smart and talented without effort or mistakes. Dweck did a study where she primed the kids for a growth mindset (before a math test, they studied mathematicians who didn't have natural talent but became great) or a fixed mindset (before the math test, they studied mathematicians who were "naturally" talented). The kids primed for a growth mindset did better, even though they had the same skills as the fixed-mindset kids.

Carol Dweck has a program for parents, educators, and students that teaches how to develop a growth mindset at *www .mindsetworks.com.* While this is a paid program, there is also a free trial for first-time users.

Dweck and other researchers have demonstrated that talents and abilities are learned and can be modified with effort. Practical applications for parents include:

○ Have a growth mindset about your child's abilities, and share stories of people who worked hard to become experts at a task or talent. Share your own stories of how you improved with practice.

○ Praise effort, not ability. Instead of "You are so smart in math!" (implication: you have to demonstrate that you are so smart in math so that you don't make mistakes), say "Look how hard you are working on those math problems!" (implication: effort pays off, and you can grow your math skills).

○ Focus on your child's personal best rather than being the best in the class. Also, don't let your child compare herself to someone who has been doing a task for a long time. Kids sometimes say things like "You're a better artist, you draw it." That inappropriate yardstick will set up a perfectionist to feel like a failure at age eight. You might respond with "I have been practicing how to draw for a long time. It's your turn to practice!"

The 1:5 Rule

Children and adolescents with executive functioning difficulties are constantly being given corrective feedback. Examples of corrective feedback include "Don't forget your homework" and "You need to check that math problem again." Positive feedback would be something like "Good job remembering your homework today" or "I like how you checked your work on that math problem to find errors." Even when corrective feedback is given in a positive tone, the child will only hear that he isn't doing things quite right, or he hasn't done quite enough to meet a standard. This can wear on a child's self-esteem, self-confidence, and optimism. Just imagine if you went to your job every day and someone was constantly directing you to do things differently!

This is why parents need to keep in mind the ratio of positive feedback to negative or corrective feedback. A general rule of thumb is 1:5—for every one comment that is corrective or negative, you should make five positive comments. This sounds easy to do, but when you take a step back, you may find that you are inadvertently doing the reverse. You can investigate what your ratio is by tracking your comments for a few hours. Every time you make a positive comment, put a small item such as a penny or paperclip in your right pocket. Every time you make a corrective comment, put a small item in your left pocket. Or you can make tally marks on paper, or put rubber bands on your wrists—any way you want to track the ratio is fine. Just check the totals at the end of a few hours to see how you are balancing out. If you are not at a 1:5 corrective-to-positive ratio, make it a point to make more positive comments about your child's performance, however small, to tip the balance in the right direction. It is important that your positive comments are sincere, as your child can see through false praise. Once you start searching for positive behaviors to note, you will likely find that there are many missed opportunities to praise your child for genuine positive behavior.

Staying positive while parenting a child with executive functioning challenges can be difficult but well worth it. You will be a happier parent and your child will be a happier child. Positive parent-child relationships set the stage for learning together, growing, and enjoying each other.

Appendix A: Developmental Tasks Requiring Executive Skills

Researchers Peg Dawson and Richard Guare have complied a list of executive functioning skills that are expected from children and adolescents at different stages of development. This table can serve as a general guide for the types of executive functioning skills to expect in your child or adolescent.

Developmental Tasks Requiring Executive Skills

Age Range	Developmental Task
Preschool	Run simple errands (e.g., "Get your shoes from the bedroom").
	Tidy bedroom or playroom with assistance.
	Perform simple chores and self-help tasks with reminders (e.g., clear dishes from table, brush teeth, get dressed).
	Inhibit behaviors: don't touch a hot stove, run into the street, grab a toy from another child, hit, bite, push, etc.
Kindergarten–Grade 2	Run errands (two- to three-step directions).
	Tidy bedroom or playroom.
	Perform simple chores, self-help tasks: may need reminders (e.g., make bed).
	Bring papers to and from school.
	Complete homework assignments (20 minutes maximum).
	Decide how to spend money (allowance).
	Inhibit behaviors: follow safety rules, don't swear, raise hand before speaking in class, keep hands to self.

Developmental Tasks Requiring Executive Skills

Age Range	Developmental Task
Grades 3–5	Run errands (may involve time delay or greater distance, such as going to a nearby store or remembering to do something after school).
	Tidy bedroom or playroom (may include vacuuming, dusting, etc.).
	Perform chores that take 15–30 minutes (e.g., clean up after dinner, rake leaves).
	Bring books, papers, assignments to and from school.
	Keep track of belongings when away from home.
	Complete homework assignments (1 hour maximum).
	Plan simple school project such as book report (select book, read book, write report).
	Keep track of changing daily schedule (i.e., different activities after school).
	Save money for desired objects, plan how to earn money.

Developmental Tasks Requiring Executive Skills

Age Range	Developmental Task
Grades 6–8	Inhibit/self-regulate: behave when teacher is out of the classroom; refrain from rude comments, temper tantrums, bad manners.
	Babysit younger siblings for pay.
	Use system for organizing schoolwork, including assignment book, notebooks, etc.
	Follow complex school schedule involving changing teachers and changing schedules.
	Plan and carry out long-term projects, including tasks to be accomplished and reasonable timeline to follow; may require planning multiple large projects simultaneously.
	Plan time, including afterschool activities, homework, family responsibilities; estimate how long it takes to complete individual tasks and adjust schedule to fit.
	Inhibit rule breaking in the absence of visible authority.

Developmental Tasks Requiring Executive Skills

Age Range	Developmental Task
High school	Manage schoolwork effectively on a day-to-day basis, including completing and handing in assignments on time, studying for tests, creating and following timelines for long-term projects, and making adjustments in effort and quality of work in response to feedback from teachers and others (e.g., grades on tests, papers).
	Establish and refine a long-term goal and make plans for meeting that goal. If the goal beyond high school is college, the youngster selects appropriate courses and maintains GPA to ensure acceptance into college. The youngster also participates in extracurricular activities, signs up for and takes SATs or ACTs at the appropriate time, and carries out the college application process. If the youngster does not plan to go to college, he or she pursues vocational courses and, if applicable, employment outside of school to ensure the training and experience necessary to obtain employment after graduation.
	Make good use of leisure time, including obtaining employment or pursuing recreational activities during the summer.
	Inhibit reckless and dangerous behaviors (e.g., use of illegal substances, sexual acting out, shoplifting, vandalism).

Table reprinted with permission from *Executive Skills in Children and Adolescents, Second Edition* by Peg Dawson and Richard Guare. © 2010.

Appendix B:
Checklists for Supporting the
"Big Ten" Executive Functions

This appendix is provided for parents to use as a "cheat sheet" for helping your child or adolescent with each of the Big Ten executive functions. The strategies from the book are organized into checklists for you to use as you target each skill area.

Strategies for Task Initiation

☐ Provide transition prompts or heads-up statements before your child is expected to start a new task.

☐ Use visual aids, such as a timer, to show young children how long they have before they need to begin a new task.

☐ Teach language concepts such as "first-then," "first-next-then," "before-after" to young children so the children can understand transitions.

☐ For young children or children with more severe transition impairments, use visual supports for transitions by showing the children pictures or photographs of the next task they are expected to do.

☐ Give specific praise when your child successfully transitions to a new task.

☐ Consider setting up a tangible reward system, such as a sticker chart, to reward your child when he does the task you ask him to do.

☐ Encourage your child to picture what it will look like to be done with a task and think about the positive emotions he will feel when it is done.

☐ Make sure your child knows how to do a task before assuming he has a problem with task initiation.

☐ Break down bigger tasks into more manageable, smaller tasks.

☐ Allow your child some choice in what task he can do first.

☐ Teach goal-setting for completing tasks and help your child reflect on what worked and what didn't for completing the task.

☐ Ensure that your child has a consistent homework routine by designating a homework space free of technological distractions, and designating a time that homework will be completed.

☐ Teach your child or adolescent about why the procrastination cycle is so powerful (to protect your ego).

☐ Teach your child or adolescent positive self-talk for task initiation. Instead of "I'll never finish this essay," teach him to say, "I will start on the topic sentence and see how it goes."

☐ Collaborate with your child or adolescent on rules about social media and technology use during homework time (for example, use only as a break, no Internet until homework is done, homework with computer use should be done in a common room, or set up a tech-free zone for homework).

Strategies for Strengthening Response Inhibition

☐ Encourage children who read impulsively and make frequent mistakes to read out loud to catch their errors.

☐ Teach self-control using fun games such as Red Light, Green Light or Simon Says.

☐ Look for your child's warning signs preceding unwanted impulsive behavior and intervene early with a desired behavior or a coping strategy.

☐ Explicitly teach your child what you want her to do ("Please wait your turn") instead of just saying what you don't want her to do ("Don't interrupt me").

☐ "Catch" your child when she is acting appropriately (being patient, asking permission to use something, or waiting her turn) and praise her immediately.

☐ Look for patterns of mistakes (adding instead of subtracting, not using punctuation in writing) in your child's schoolwork and talk with your child's teachers about strategies to help with that type of mistake.

☐ Teach sequences or learning routines that your child can use to check her own work for mistakes.

☐ For homework assignments, teach your child how to read directions thoroughly. Talk it out with her to ensure that she knows all of the steps involved.

☐ Teach your child color-coding and highlighting strategies to draw attention to important information in worksheets, homework, or reading assignments.

Focus Strategies

☐ Explicitly teach your child what focus looks like by telling him what behaviors you see when he is focused: eyes on work, feet and body still, etc.

☐ To teach self-regulation of focus, consider using a timer at random intervals and when the timer goes off, have your child report whether he was focused.

☐ When your child has several tasks to complete, allow him some choice in what he has to focus on first.

- [ ] Encourage your child to focus on one task at a time. Share the research with him that multitasking affects learning and grades in a negative way.
- [ ] Set up ground rules about media-free study time. Use media as a break, rather than have it available as a source of distraction.
- [ ] Turn off the TV during study or homework time. Even background TV can deflect focus.
- [ ] Limit music when your child has to focus on something cognitively challenging. If he insists on having music, choose music without vocals.
- [ ] Encourage and teach your child mindfulness—the practice of focusing on one thing for a period of time, whether it be on the breath, a mantra, or a visualization.

Time Management Strategies

- [ ] To facilitate good time management when getting ready to leave the house, help your child visualize what "ready" looks like.
- [ ] Encourage your child to conjure up her "ready" image before you ask her to get ready.
- [ ] For a younger child, you may want to take a photograph of what "ready" looks like and reference it the next time you ask her to get ready.
- [ ] Teach your child to think in categories of what she needs to be ready instead of in checklists. Categories may include personal hygiene, food, school supplies, personal items, and afterschool activities.
- [ ] Encourage your child to get items needed for the next day ready to go the night before.
- [ ] To keep your child from getting distracted during meals, enforce a ground rule that there are no toys or electronics at the table.
- [ ] Have your child make predictions about how long each homework task will take and check in afterward to see how long it actually took. Discuss the patterns you see with her.
- [ ] Have your child use an analog clock rather than a digital clock at her homework area. You can have her put a Post-it on the time she needs to work until so she can visualize and begin to have a better sense of passing time.

- [ ] Help your child break big tasks into manageable parts and estimate how long each part will take.
- [ ] Some children will prefer a "beat the clock" game in which a kitchen timer is set and they work until the timer goes off and evaluate how far they got.
- [ ] Teach your child how to use a planner, whether it be a written one or a technological one.
- [ ] Post a family calendar and refer to it to teach planning and time management skills.

Strategies for Boosting Working Memory

- [ ] Have your child repeat back directions to you to check for understanding.
- [ ] Shorten complex directions by providing steps one at a time.
- [ ] Teach your child to write down the steps in lengthy directions, either on paper or in an electronic device.
- [ ] Encourage exercise and mindfulness practices, both of which improve memory.
- [ ] Prime your child's memory by telling him what to listen for before you give a direction or information.
- [ ] Teach memory strategies such as chunking information (thinking of information in categories rather than individually), mnemonics, and associations (clever ways to remember information).
- [ ] Help your child remember better by encouraging multisensory studying techniques, such as pairing visual and auditory information together.
- [ ] For rote memorization, teach your child how to use flashcards or online games such as Quizlet that will build recall, not just recognition.
- [ ] Encourage your child to make a study guide by reviewing his notes, textbooks, and supplementary materials and, with your help, pulling out important concepts.
- [ ] Teach the memory strategy of elaboration, which is linking new information to something he already knows.

Strategies for Improving Flexibility

- [ ] Introduce the concept of rebooting with your child when she gets stuck on an ineffective strategy for solving a problem or is fixated on an idea about how things should be done. Encourage her to take a break and reboot.
- [ ] Teach calming strategies your child can use during reboot breaks, such as deep breathing, taking a short walk, doing a mindfulness activity, or listening to a favorite song.
- [ ] Teach your child feeling vocabulary, and help her label her feelings when she is stuck.
- [ ] Teach self-talk and thought-stopping techniques for when your child gets stuck. For example, change "should" statements to "sometimes" statements.
- [ ] Read stories about children who are flexible thinkers and discuss them with your child.
- [ ] For children who get upset when there is a change, provide anticipatory guidance or a heads-up if there is a known change in schedule so they can mentally prepare for it.
- [ ] Make small, manageable changes and teach your child how to cope with them. This will prepare her for bigger changes.
- [ ] If your child has a meltdown about a change or because she wasn't able to do things her way, calm her down and then later discuss the event, the feelings, and what she could do differently next time.

Self-Regulation Strategies

- [ ] In reading, teach your child to visualize what he is reading while he is reading. He might picture it as a movie, or draw what he read, for example. If he can't picture it, he may not have read correctly or remembered what he read.
- [ ] Teach your child how to make personal connections to what he has read. Older children can be encouraged to make connections between other things they have read or events in the world. You can have your child write down his connections or tell them to you.
- [ ] Teach your child to ask questions about what he wants to learn and the purpose of the reading assignment before he reads to help him focus.

- [ ] Your child can also ask clarifying questions during the reading process, either by writing them down or by having a discussion with you.
- [ ] For younger children, encourage them to make predictions about what will happen next in the book. Teach them how to look for clues about what is to come and make guesses together and check your guesses.
- [ ] Teach good prewriting strategies by discussing the topic first. Ask your child what he already knows about the topic, questions he may have, and ideas for writing. From there, you can teach him how to make an outline, or encourage him to create a graphic organizer.
- [ ] To counteract writer's block, teach your child to do a prewriting activity called mental contrasting, in which the child writes about the process he will undergo when writing. Then, he develops a plan for overcoming any obstacles for completing the writing task.
- [ ] Ask your child's teacher for examples of model writing in the genre in which your child has to write. Go over the core features of the genre and help your child understand the parts he will have to do.
- [ ] Ask your child's teacher if there are rubrics for written work. This way you and your child will know what aspects of writing are being focused on and what he will eventually be graded on. This gives structure and a guideline for the writing piece.
- [ ] Teach your child the organizational strategy of putting writing ideas on cards and then physically organizing them into groups by theme to develop main ideas connected to a thesis.
- [ ] Practice basic math facts in a fun way, such as with online games, apps, and by making math musical.
- [ ] Help your child break down a math problem into manageable steps and emphasize and discuss each step as you go through it.
- [ ] Teach problem-solving sequences that help kids talk through the steps needed to do a problem. One such sequence is the "Understand, plan, do, and check" sequence.
- [ ] Utilize online learning tools targeted to math concepts that your child is struggling with.

☐ Understand the connection between play and self-regulation. Encourage your young child to engage in make-believe play and imaginative play. You may even make a "play plan" with your child and talk about the materials needed for the play and the roles that you will take on.

Teaching Emotional Self-Control

☐ Teach your child more than just basic feeling vocabulary, like *sad*, *mad*, *happy*, or *scared*. Teach the range of emotions and nuanced emotion words as well (*annoyed* versus *furious*).

☐ Model emotional regulation by labeling your own feelings out loud and discussing how you will cope with them.

☐ Teach feeling vocabulary through books by discussing the feelings the characters had and asking your child to make connections to her own experiences.

☐ When you see your child experiencing an emotion, you can help build awareness of feelings by labeling it for her. Using the notice-and-explore technique, you can gently help your child understand what she is feeling ("I noticed that when you couldn't get a cookie you tore up my papers. I am wondering if you might be frustrated, disappointed, or angry. Can you tell me more about what you are thinking about?").

☐ If your child acts out when experiencing a strong emotion, label it, validate it, and then provide a clear direction about what she should do instead of the negative behavior.

☐ If your child is having an outburst, model calmness and use a firm and confident voice to correct the behavior.

☐ Check in frequently with your child about how she is feeling. You may want to track feelings and chart them together to build awareness of the connections between events, thoughts, feelings, and behaviors.

☐ Teach family rules such as being safe, responsible, and respectful and remind your child of the rule when it is broken. Also, you can praise your child when she manages her emotions well and exhibits behavior that follows the family rules. This will help her become more aware of her feelings and behavior.

- ☐ Know your child's triggers or predictors for emotional or behavioral reactions. When you see a trigger, try the notice-and-explore technique and encourage a coping strategy to ward off a full-blown reaction.
- ☐ Punishment for inappropriate behavior should be a natural consequence, not arbitrary.

Techniques for Teaching Task Completion

- ☐ For short-term tasks, encourage your child to picture the end result of doing the task and the positive emotion that may be attached to it.
- ☐ Present the idea of chores as tasks that are done to show respect for your family and pride in your responsibility. Provide rationales for each chore.
- ☐ Provide a visual of all the chores for each family member and give your child or children some choice in which ones they would like to be responsible for.
- ☐ Make sure your child can do a chore independently, or teach him the steps needed to do it.
- ☐ Try to make a game out of chores, or brainstorm with your child or adolescent on ways to make chores less mundane.
- ☐ Discuss the quality expectation of chores before asking your kids to complete them.
- ☐ Break apart big chores into a series of smaller parts.
- ☐ Consider using a rewards chart for successful chore completion.
- ☐ Hold consistent expectations about when, where, and how homework is done in your household.
- ☐ Designate a homework time based on your child's energy level and rhythms.
- ☐ Set up a work area for your child that is not distracting and encourage or enforce that homework be completed in that area. The area should be free of TV and technology.
- ☐ Make a plan about how homework time will be spent by looking over what your child has to do that evening and what is on-deck and together come up with the order of the tasks and time estimations. Reflect on the homework process when it is completed.

- [ ] You may need to help your child schedule breaks or mini-rewards during lengthy homework sessions.
- [ ] Create goal charts with your child to track success. You may build in rewards for when he reaches his goals. Rewards do not have to be purchased; they can be extension of privileges, for example.
- [ ] Break long reading assignments into smaller, more manageable parts and make a reading schedule together.
- [ ] When teachers assign a certain amount of time your child must read per night, create a reading log or chart that your child can mark when he finishes his reading session.
- [ ] Explore modifications and accommodations that may be available to your child, such as getting reading assignments in advance or downloading an audiobook version for your child to listen to and follow along in the book.
- [ ] For long-term projects, help your child see the long view by taking each task and putting it on a calendar with a series of interim due dates.

Supporting Organization Skills

- [ ] Teach your child the mantra "Everything has a home" for remembering to put belongings in their proper place.
- [ ] Use labels or pictures of items as visual reminders of where items belong.
- [ ] Designate a specific daily time when your child is to de-clutter a space.
- [ ] Help your child with larger de-cluttering projects by teaching her how to get rid of things in a systematic way—for example, sorting items into three baskets: throw away, give away, and store.
- [ ] Apply the "Everything has a home" technique for backpacks as well. Help your child designate spaces in the backpack for certain items.
- [ ] Consider getting a second set of textbooks to keep at home so your child does not have to remember which textbooks to bring home each day.

- [ ] Set a backpack-cleaning routine, perhaps when your child first comes home from school. Ask her questions about where things go and her system for filing rather than organizing it for her.
- [ ] Help your child come up with a system for filing school papers. Ask questions about what her system is so you can help her streamline it. Help your child make decisions about which papers she needs to keep and which can be recycled.
- [ ] Help your child color-code each school subject and use that color for all the materials related to that subject.
- [ ] For homework papers, help your child make a "do-done" folder, where she puts homework she has to do on one side and completed homework on the other.
- [ ] Encourage the use of a planner. Help your child find the planner that best suits her needs, though one that has a week- or month-at-a-glance function is preferred over a daily one so she can see what is coming up. Frequently check in to see if your child is using her planner, and enlist the help of her teacher or teachers to check as well, if possible.
- [ ] To help your child remember core items she always needs, have a "home" for these items and help your child make a short checklist of items needed every day (phone, keys, wallet/purse).
- [ ] To remember items that your child doesn't need every day, encourage her to take a mental picture of what she needs by category (sports equipment, school items, food items) and compare it with what she has actually gathered to take with her.
- [ ] Teach your child to "Do the spin" after she leaves a space and check for items she would have otherwise forgotten.

Index